THE MILITARY SPOUSE

The Military Spouse Y0-CKO-401

COPYRIGHT MENTOR PUBLICATIONS LLC

All rights reserved. No part of this publication may be reproduced or transmitted in any form or by any means, electronic or mechanical, including photocopy, recording or any information storage and retrieval system, without the expressed permission in writing from the publisher.

"The views expressed in this book are those of the Mentor Publications (LLC) and do not reflect the official policy or position of the Army, Defense Department or the United States Government. No copyrights are claimed on material created by the United States Government.

All Rights Reserved
2006-2009

Published by:

MENTOR ENTERPRISES, INC.
7910 Memorial Parkway
Huntsville, Alabama 35802
256-885-3535
Fax: 256-885-3531
info@mentorenterprisesinc.com

PATRICIA GERECHT & MARK GERECHT

WARNING - DISCLAIMER

This product is designed to provide a source of information concerning the subject matter. It is sold with the understanding that the Corporation (Mentor Publications) and its employees, agents, authors, editors and publisher are not providing any legal or any other type of professional service. If legal services/opinions or any other type of professional service is required, the reader should seek guidance from a competent professional.

The content of this product is compilation of information gathered from Military manuals, personal experience of the contributors, and editors. The samples in this product are suggestions, not exact models. Readers should consult regulatory guides for specifics. This product is a guide. **It does not** in any way take precedence over military regulation or local policies and procedures. In all cases for the purpose of this product military regulation and local policies are considered the governing sources. **Readers** should not take any action based on information contained in this product but should research their specific questions thru military manuals or professionals.

Every effort was made to ensure that this product was complete, accurate at the time of printing. *It is possible that mistakes may be found both in content and typography*. This product should be used only as a **guide** and not as the source or ultimate authority.

The purpose of the product is to educate and entertain only. The authors, agents, editors, or publisher shall have no liability or responsibility to any person or entity concerning loss/damage alleged, to be caused or caused by any means directly or indirectly by the information in this product.

The authors encourage and welcome comments, suggestions, ideas, or questions at:

mentorpubs@bellsouth.net

All material will be reviewed for possible use in future printings.
Please provide your e-mail address and phone number with your correspondence.

In this product the term "commander" refers to commanders at all levels. Some commanders have different levels of authority. The local policy on the authority of a commander should be checked in your area. In addition, any reference to the term "he" should be understood to include both genders.

THE MILITARY SPOUSE

Other publications available from

Books

THE MENTOR: *Everything You Need To Know About Leadership and Counseling.*

THE TRAINER: *A Training Guide for All Ranks.*

THE EVALUATOR: *A Comprehensive Guide for Preparing NCOER Evaluation Reports.*

THE WRITER: *A comprehensive guide for writing awards.*

Wear It Right! Army Uniform Book: *Answer your army uniform questions instantly!*

Digital Products

Award Quick: *Helps you quickly and accurately write the awards your soldiers deserve. Includes citations, achievement statements, forms, and much more.*

Counsel Quick: *Innovative software that includes all the forms, examples, and references you will need to quickly compose and manage US Army counseling statements.*

Counsel Quick Vol. 1: *Places special emphasis on counseling typically conducted by first line leaders.*

Counsel Quick Vol. 2: *Places special emphasis on counseling typically conducted by senior leaders.*

Counsel Quick Vol. 3: *Even more counseling templates and references! Available July 2009.*

Rater Quick: *Contains the latest forms, examples, and references you will need to quickly compose and manage professional looking Evaluation Reports all in one easy to use program. We offer both OER and NCOER versions of this software.*

Also available online at www.gipubs.com.

3

Dedication

**To the amazing men and women
who keep the home front running smoothly
so that our service members
can defend our way of life.**

GOD BLESS OUR MILITARY SPOUSES!

**Last but not least we thank God for
our wonderful daughter Shania
and our parents.**

Our goals are

- to make this the most comprehensive spouse book available for all the armed services, and
- provide down to earth guidance on everyday issues.

Help us, help others by sending your comments, suggestions and ideas to:

mentorpubs@bellsouth.net

Please provide your contact information in the email.

CONTRIBUTORS

A special thanks to the following individuals for providing their information, material, thoughts, advice, and feedback so that we could make this book better for all military spouses:

- Mrs. Becky Pillsbury
- Mrs. Marilyn Phillips
- Col Sam and Alicia Liburdi, USAF, Ret.
- **Major Larry and Michaela Cannon** (Former Co CDR & FRG Leader)
- **AKCM (R) Roy and Mr. Roy Callahan** (USN)
- **CSM John and Mrs. Brenda Perry** (United States Army Reserve/ FRG Leaders)
- **SFC (R) David and Judy Carney** (Alabama National Guard)
- **Luis Muniz** (Financial Planner)
- **Sue Paddock** (Army Community Service Director)
- **Ms. Sarah Brazzel** (Protocol Advisor)
- **Major Joey Byrd** (Chaplain Advisor)

Book Editor: Jennifer Devlin

Table of Contents

CHAPTER 1 "Introduction" — 13

CHAPTER 2 "Financial Matters" — 15

    Military Consequences for Failing to Pay Debts — 15
    Dealing With Merchants — 16
    Off Limits Lists — 16
    If the Creditors Start Calling — 16
    Debt Spending Habits — 18
    Help With a Budget — 22
    Reduced Interest Rates — 22
    Soldier/Sailors Relief Act — 23
    Ways to Save for Success — 26
    How to Read a Leave and Earnings Statement (LES) — 29
    Deployments — 30
    Reduce Taxes — 30
    Debt Consolidation — 32
    Bankruptcy — 32
    Divorces — 33
    Credit Scores — 34
    Other Sources of Employment — 36
    Emergency Fund — 36
    The Act of Giving — 36
    Investing — 37
    Identity Theft — 41
    Spouse Unemployment resulting from PCS — 49

CHAPTER 3 "Our Children & Money" — 51

    Teach Children to Save — 51
    Giving More Than We Can Afford — 51
    Latest & Greatest — 51
    Model Behavior — 51
    Chores — 51
    Charity, Spending, & Savings — 52
    Education — 52

401P (Parent Fund)	52
Brand Names	53

CHAPTER 4 "Buying a Home" — 55

Before You Buy	55
Mortgages	56
Get Pre-approved	57
How Much House Should We Buy	57
House Inspections	57
Ways to Prepare on Your Mortgage	57
Are You Planning to Build	58

CHAPTER 5 "Insurance" — 61

Life	61
SGLI	62
Credit	62
Auto	63
Home/Renters	64
Discounts	65
Disability/Cancer	65
Long Term Care	66

CHAPTER 6 "The Do's and Don'ts of Social Graces For a Military Spouse" — 69

Tips	69
Key Terms	74
Rules for a Receiving Line	75
Teas/Coffees	75
How Should I Eat That	78
How Should I Dress	78
Invitations	84
Thank You Notes	85
Example Thank You	86

THE MILITARY SPOUSE

CHAPTER 7 "Dealing With Deployments"	87
Support Agencies	87
How to Cope	92
Dealing with Deployments	94
National Guard & Reserves	96
CHAPTER 8 "Honey, It's Time to Move"	99
Hold Baggage	99
Household Goods	100
Storage	100
Do It Yourself Move (DITY)	101
Moving Planner Checklist	102
Tips for Moving	107
Move Out Day	112
Move In Day	113
Money & Moving	114
Regulations	116
Inprocessing	116
Travel Time	116
Types of Leave	116
De Junking Day	117
Hitting the Road	118
Types of Travel	119
Making a House a Home	119
Homeowners Assistance Program (HAP)	120
CHAPTER 9 "Hey! What About My Career"	121
Types of Government Jobs	121
Non Government Jobs	122
Private Industry	123
Home Business	125
Temporary Hire Agencies	125
Volunteering	125
Preparing for a Job	126
Tips in Looking for a Job	134

Education 135

CHAPTER 10 "Family Matters" 137

    Lautenberg Amendment 138
    Keep Your Private Life Private 139
    Prenuptial Agreements 140
    Divorce 140
    Money and Marriage 141

CHAPTER 11 "Preparing for the Future" 143

    Wills 144
    Executor (Appointing) 145
    Letter of Instruction 145
    Living Will 148
    Death Benefits 149
    Getting Organized 150
    Potential Benefits 150
    Stoppage of Active Duty Benefits 150
    Service Members Group Life Insurance (SGLI) 151
    Traumatic Service Members Group Life Insurance
       (TSGLI) 151
    Family Service Members Group Life Insurance (FSGLI) ... 152
    Death Gratuity 152
    Death/Burial 153
    Burial for Spouses and Dependents 153
    Persons Not Eligible 154
    Health Benefits 156
    Basic Allowance for Housing 157
    Federal Employment 157
    State Benefits 158
    Unpaid Compensation 158
    ID Card 158
    Victim Assistance Program 159
    Survivors Benefit Plan 160
    Reserve Component Survivors Benefit Plan 160
    Dependency and Indemnity Compensation (DIC) Offset ... 161
    Non Service Connected Death 163

THE MILITARY SPOUSE

Educational Benefit Assistance	163
Social Security	165
Commissary Privileges	167
Base Exchange Privileges	167
Emergency Financial Assistance	167
Income Tax	167
Commercial Life Insurance	168
Required Documents	168
VA Home Loan	168
Bank Accounts	168
Military Funeral Support	169
Frequently Asked Questions (Funerals)	170

CHAPTER 12 "How to Voice Your Concerns, Opinions,
　　　　　　Complaints and be Heard" 　　　　　175

Attitude and Tone	175
Goals	175
Steps to Resolving a Concern or Issue	176
Other Channels for Resolution	179
Do's	180
Avoids	180
Common Sense Check	181
Family Support Chain	182

CHAPTER 13 "Important Websites and Agencies"　　　183

CHAPTER 14　Military Rank Insignias of Grade for all Services　　193

Army, Air Force & Marine Officer Ranks	193
Navy & Coast Guard Officer Ranks	194
Army Warrant Officer Ranks	195
Navy Warrant Officer Ranks	196
Marine Warrant Officer Ranks	196
Coast Guard Warrant Officer Ranks	197
Army Enlisted Ranks	198
Air Force Enlisted Ranks	199
Marine Enlisted Ranks	200
Navy Enlisted Ranks	201

Coast Guard Enlisted Ranks   202

CHAPTER 1
INTRODUCTION

The information contained in this book represents over 200 years of experience and has been compiled from the life experiences of numerous military spouses and active duty service members from several of the armed services. This book is designed as a "welcome to your new life" or "a Military 101 self help book". It contains situations you may encounter on a daily basis and is designed to be as user friendly as possible.

Chances are if you are reading this book you are either newly married to a soldier, airman, marine, sailor, or member of the Coast Guard: your spouse has changed careers and is now a member of the armed services, you wanted more information on the military, or you wanted to learn the ropes of being a supportive spouse. As the spouse and someone who supports a service member, your life will be both rewarding and challenging.

You will more than likely experience travel to other countries, different cultures, learn how to deal with the day to day challenges of military culture and how to handle family, financial, and a vast array of other issues when your spouse is deployed or on extended training. Either way your experience will be one filled with adventure. The adventure of your military experience can be as positive as you make it, and our goal is to ensure we provide you with necessary information to help you adjust, understand, and most importantly, enjoy the military experience.

Whether your tour in the military (Active, Reserve, or National Guard) is a 2 year enlistment or a 30 year career there is much to learn and the opportunities are boundless. You will experience moments of overwhelming joy, times of utter frustration, and at times you may even experience loneliness. You and your family and military unit may even grieve the loss of a service member.

The wonderful part about the military is that, for the most part, it is a group of individuals who share a common bond and many seasoned spouses will be able to prepare and assist you as you come to know the military system.

This book has been designed so that it hits the basics that most military spouses will experience. *It does have an Army flavor* to it but each service offers regulations, instructions, and services very similar to the Army, therefore you should have no problem finding assistance within these pages. We encourage you to use the internet, your specific military service regulations/instructions, and support agencies to gain a better understanding of how your specific service is set up to assist spouses and family members. **Some service specific web addresses you may find useful are: US ARMY: www.army.mil, Marines: www.USMC.mil, Navy: www.navy.mil, Air Force: www.af.mil, Coast Guard: www.uscg.mil**

Remember we are all in this together and by sharing common solutions to common issues we strengthen our fighting force and allow the service member to focus on the mission. Please sit back and enjoy the book… we hope you find the information useful and inspirational.

Last but not least we would greatly appreciate any comments, suggestions, or ideas you may have that may improve this product. **Your words of wisdom and personal experience will be invaluable to other military spouses!**

Please send all your comments, suggestions and feedback to the authors at: ***mentorpubs@bellsouth.net***

THE MILITARY SPOUSE

CHAPTER 2
FINANCIAL MATTERS

Being a Soldier, Sailor, Airman, Marine, or member of the Coast Guard is not exactly the best paid job in the world! Even still, joining the military is perhaps one of the most selfless and honorable commitments an individual can make. As military spouses, we are usually the individuals responsible for making sure the bills are paid and the households are maintained, along with taking care of the family and/or working outside the home. Typically our military spouses work long hours or are deployed for long periods of time. Therefore, it is imperative that we manage our money wisely. We also benefit from teaching our children at a young age how to manage money in a manner that will provide them a better standard of living. This chapter will focus on military pay and benefits, as well as methods to establish, improve, and grow your assets.

Military Consequences For Failing To Pay Debts: A major factor effecting military families today is financial debt. Living within our means is the best way to prepare for and safeguard our future and that of our children. While civilians face certain penalties for not paying their bills, a service member faces additional consequences. A military commander may punish a service member under the Uniform Code of Military Justice for failing to pay a just debt. Depending on the level of punishment, a military member could lose 7-30 days pay, lose one or more grades of rank, and be ordered to perform additional work after the normal duty day (normally called extra duty). In addition, failing to pay a debt also has an impact on the credibility of a service member and can have a negative impact on the image of the service. Finally, neglecting to pay off debts can have a negative impact on the service member's security clearance. In a nutshell, failing to pay a debt impacts the service member and their family. As a spouse we should do everything we can to work with our service members in managing financial matters.

Dealing with Merchants: When dealing with merchants you should do your best to deal with reputable vendors. There are agencies close to military installations that look for inexperienced or desperate individuals and families. These institutions will normally charge **very high interest rates** for services rendered. Some of these services may include: payday advances, car titles for cash, furniture/appliance financing, or used car lots. If you need money badly enough, someone is willing to take advantage of you or your family so **READ THE FINE PRINT**. Look at the interest rate you are being charged! In addition, some companies will have a **waiver in their contract** that states they can contact your employer should you not pay your bill on time. **Do not sign such waivers**. It is better to save for what you want than to pay significantly higher interest rates. While the command wants all military members to pay their debts, they do not want them to receive poor quality or overpriced services. We strongly encourage that you never put your car title up for cash!

Off Limits List: Ensure the business you are dealing with has not been placed off limits by the post commander. Agencies placed off limits by the post commander are usually posted on bulletin boards and can be obtained at the local Judge Advocate General (JAG) office. They have been placed off limits because they have displayed practices which take advantage of military members or their families.

If The Creditors Start Calling: Creditors cannot harass you at work nor can they contact your employer unless you have given them expressed permission. If you are having difficulty with creditors contact your local legal assistance office immediately. We suggest that you reference **Army Regulation 600-15,** Indebtness of Military Personnel, **Air Force Instruction 36-2906,** Personal Financial Responsibility, and **Department of Defense Directive 1344.9** Indebtedness of Military Personnel (contained on the CD). (E*ach service will have a corresponding regulation or instruction on this matter.*, Chapter 4 of AR 600-15 spells out the requirements a creditor must meet and how they must proceed in accordance with the Fair Debt Collection Act, and the

THE MILITARY SPOUSE

Truth in Lending Act. **Debt Collectors are required by law to provide certain forms under the fair debt collection act and failing to do so may be in violation of your rights.** We bring this to your attention in the event that you are being treated unfairly or harassed. **However, it is imperative that you pay (Actual or True) debts in a timely manner.** Failure to pay a debt could result in adverse action being taken against the service member. If you believe you are being pursued by a debt collector or harassed at work, immediately inform the chain of command and seek guidance from an attorney at the JAG office. **Do not keep the problem from the Chain of Command.** They are normally your best link to solving a financial problem. They can refer you to professionals trained in dealing with debt collectors, put you in contact with agencies that can provide budget counseling, investment counseling, and work to provide financial aid in the form of interest free loans or grants (if needed), they may also be able to arrange for food in emergencies. *Most senior enlisted leaders have experienced some type of financial hardships during their early years in the services…***they understand**…but they must be kept informed. Author Dave Ramsey, in his book Financial Peace Planner, offers the following information concerning the Fair Debt Collection Act: He states that in 1977 Congress passed a law called the Fair Debt Collection Act that makes the following stipulations:

- Collectors can call only between the hours of 8 am and 9 pm unless you have given them permission to do otherwise.

- You can keep creditors from calling you at work. You should do this in writing and be sure to send the letter by certified mail, return receipt requested. This way you know when the creditor received your letter and you know if they are breaking the law.

- You can demand that creditors stop all contact except to notify you of legal proceedings. Do this in writing but only as a last resort…this can make the collector mad… not a good move if you are trying to work with them…(as stated by Ramsey).

- Collectors and creditors cannot confiscate a bank account or garnish wages without suing you and winning the case.

Please keep in mind rules/laws change so do your research and seek legal advice from the local legal assistance office.

How To Get Out Of Debt And Control Spending Habits: Perhaps the best way is to sit down and take note of how you are spending your money. Are you spending money on things that you really don't need? Remember there is a difference between a *need* (required for living) and a *want* (nice to have). For instance:

- Are you spending $65 a month for satellite TV or cable? Do you really need it? Could you **go without satellite TV or cable** and simply use local channels? Sure you could....WOW you just freed up $65!

- **Do you have a cell phone** or two and a home phone? Do you need both? How high is your long distance bill? Consider having long distance removed from your home phone and just go with local service. Another option is to get an unlimited long distance calling plan instead of a by the minute rate plan or utilize calling cards for long distance calls. When calling card minutes are used, you are done with your long distance calls until the next payday. How about removing features you don't use or need like call waiting, call forwarding, or caller ID? Consider dropping one or both of your cell phones. Figure out what you really need, and go with that. Understand that termination of a cell phone contract may hurt initially but it will save you in the long run. WOW you probably just saved between $30-$100!

- **Utilize coupons** for food shopping. Most commissaries, newspapers, internet sites, and some Army Community Service (*or sister service equivalent organization*) offices offer a coupon section or coupon sharing program. The key is to use coupons for things you will actually use. *It's not a deal if it's on sale and you* *won't use it.* While this takes some time, planning and organization, it can save you realistically $40-$160 a month on your food bill. If you are stationed overseas or OCONUS (outside the continental United States), coupons are good for six months past their expiration date.

- o Look into couponing websites like couponmom.com or

- **Plan your meals**: plan meals on a weekly basis, and buy food to last for one week. You will have all the ingredients for your meals and you can eat what you have planned any time during the week. This can bring a savings of between $50-$100 a month!

- **Consider planting a garden** or using pots on your porch to grow vegetables. This will save on your fresh vegetable bill in the summer, which at times can be expensive. Freeze your vegetables for use in the winter/fall.

- Consider **buying a vacuum sealer** and place leftovers in single serving packages, or when you make a lot of something, seal it and put it in the freezer for future use. Freeze leftover vegetables and add chicken or beef stock to make a great and inexpensive soup once a week. By the way, it's also healthy!

- Always **eat before you shop**: this helps prevent impulse buying and take a list and stick to it!

- **Consider taking larger deductibles on your insurance policies** like auto and home. Taking a larger deductible *(one you can afford to pay)* will drastically reduce your insurance premium. While we are talking about insurance for automobiles and your home - do not go with the cheapest or lowest level of coverage. If you are ever in an accident and you are only carrying the minimum coverage you may be liable, if at fault for the remainder of the damage. We would also strongly encourage you to get **under insured motorist insurance** (protects you if you are in an accident and the other driver does not have enough insurance) and **uninsured motorist insurance** (in case you are hit by a driver who has no insurance). Both of these have been lifesavers for us personally, and the last thing you need during a crisis is to be worried about how you will pay for damage to a vehicle or individuals who were injured in your car.

- **When buying a car:** Are you going to buy a car you can afford or one you want? Remember cars depreciate quickly. Our recommendation is to buy a car that is 1-2 years old, usually one that was on a lease program. You can do an internet search for a small fee with the Vehicle Identification Number (VIN) to determine if the vehicle has ever been in an accident or flood. In addition, we suggest that you utilize *Consumer Reports Magazine* to check the test results listed in the magazine, and buy a car that has a dependable record as a used car. This is an invaluable tool. Your savings potential is significant. In addition, by purchasing a used car, you will also save money on car insurance.

    - ***Beware of vehicles that may have been damaged during floods like KATRINA and RITA that hit during 2005.*** *Thousands of vehicles were bought out of the affected area and refurbished to be sold as used cars.* If it is a used car check the carpet does it all look like it has been replaced? This could be a sign of flood damage. Run a VIN number search see if it contains any useful information regarding storm damage. You must be cautious when buying a used car. If the car is cheap and it is new, there is probably a good reason for it!

    - *Buying a new car might have benefits exceeding a used car purchase* if the following options on a new car are being offered: rebates, no interest (for a period of time) loans, and/ or no down payment. Leasing a vehicle usually not a good idea especially for a military member because you may be subject to movement with little notification to an overseas assignment, and you could incur a large penalty for breaking the lease.

- o You may also have the ability to register your car in your home of record which may be cheaper and you may avoid a higher tax for your tags by doing this. Also check and see if the state you are currently serving in has an exception for military members.

- o *Last but not least, remember to* **remove any Department of Defense sticker** from your vehicle prior to selling it. It is a security risk and you are liable for any misuse of decal privileges by the new owner if the sticker is left on the vehicle.

- **Don't utilize department store or special credit cards:** Most of these credit cards have high interest rates attached to them…some as high as 21%. If you decide to get a credit card, get one from a credit union or other institution that will usually have an interest rate below 10%. There are some exceptions, but read the fine print before you commit. In addition, make sure that you look for a credit card that has a *fixed rate and not a variable rate.*

- **Nights out and babysitting:** Everyone needs time away! It's important to spend time alone with your spouse, and to have conversations on an adult level. How do we do this and keep the cost low? One option is to make an agreement with another couple you trust, and offer to watch each other's children one evening every other weekend. Then you and your spouse can perhaps sit at home, have a quiet dinner and relax and watch a movie together, and they can also do the same on a different evening. This keeps the "date night" cost low and there is no charge for babysitting. You simply return the favor the following weekend for the other couple. This is a simple yet effective approach and allows you to spend two evenings a month with your spouse enjoying quality time. When it's your turn to watch their children you simply turn that into a night of fun and games for the whole family. Now you have two times a month to enjoy each other and two times a month to have a great and inexpensive family get together. A little popcorn, a board game, or a sports game in the front yard, or perhaps some time in the park with your family. These methods cut down on expense and definitely add quality time. *Planning a date night with your spouse enhances the closeness of your relationship too!*

Budget Bottom Line: Make a list of things you need and would like to have. Then prioritize them to determine what you really need and can afford. After you have done this it's time to come up with a plan to achieve your priorities. *For example: get out of debt, start a savings account, and begin an automatic payroll deduction for savings. Pay yourself first...make your monthly savings a bill you must pay. When you think of it as a bill you will begin to save for your future and it will become a habit.*

Need Help Putting Together A Budget? Visit your local Army Community Service (ACS), Air Force Family Services or equivalent service provider for the Navy, Marines, or Coast Guard. They can assist you in developing a budget and help you to work with creditors by coming up with a payment plan. We cannot stress to you the value of ACS when it comes to financially helping service members and their families. In some cases Army Emergency Relief (*each sister service has its own equivalent to AER like the Air Force Aid Society*) may be able to help with an interest free loan or a grant.

Financial Peace University: Dave Ramsey offers a program that teaches you about finances in depth. It is an exceptional program. You can usually find it being taught at churches and other organizations within your community. You can also find it at Daveramsey.com

Reduced Interest Rates: In some cases, such as deployments, you may be able to get your interest rates reduced for the duration of your deployment. Contact your creditors and they can provide you with the

THE MILITARY SPOUSE

required forms to have your interest rates reduced. Usually this applies to deployments at sea and short tours of one year to locations like Korea or combat zones.

Soldier And Sailors Relief Act: In some cases you may be eligible for protection under the Soldier and Sailors Relief Act. This applies to active service members and Reserve service members when activated. It is best to seek advice from ACS and the legal office on post. The following is an extract of an article titled "Soldiers' and Sailors' Civil Relief Act Provides Umbrella of Protection". The article was found on the website: www.defenselink.mil.

The *Soldier's and Sailors Civil Relief* Act may provide the following assistance:

- Reduced interest rate on mortgage payments.

- Reduced interest rates on credit card debt.

- Protection from eviction if your rent is $1,200 or less. If you rent a house or apartment and the rent does not exceed $1,200 per month, the landlord must obtain a court order authorizing eviction. This applies whether the quarters were rented before or after entry into military service. In cases of eviction courts may grant a stay of up to three months or enter any other order as may be just. This provision is *not* intended to allow military members to avoid paying rent; but rather, to protect families when they cannot pay rent because military service has affected their ability to pay.

- Delay of all civil court actions, such as: bankruptcy, foreclosure or divorce proceedings.

- All service members receive some protection under this act. Additional protections are available to Reserve Components called to active duty.

- One of the most significant provisions under the act limits the amount of interest that may be collected on debts of persons in military service to 6 percent per year during the period of military service. It applies to all debts incurred prior to the commencement of active duty and includes interest on credit card debt, mortgages, car loans, and other debts. The interest rate cap does not apply to federal guaranteed student loans, but the Department of Education has deferred or suspended payments on student loans for reserve component members called to active duty. Service members should contact their lender or schools to determine if such a program has been implemented and its eligibility requirements. *Upon receiving notification of deployment, or in the case of National Guard or Reserves Component service members, send all your creditors a letter stating the fact that you are deploying or being activated. Consider including a copy of your orders and request that interest rate be dropped in accordance with the Soldier's Sailors Relief Act and you may also even consider asking them if they would consider 0% interest during this time frame. They do have the option to reduce it below 6%, so why not ask? Just do it in a professional and kind manner. The worst they can say is no and that they will only give you 6%. Who knows, maybe they will drop it below 6%. You have nothing to lose so ask!*

- Repossessions: The Act prohibits repossessions performed without a court order by the merchant or REPO specialist as long as the purchase was made before active duty began. Merchants must obtain a court order before they can repo an item. If this happens the active duty service member may apply for a stay of repossession proceedings. *Contact your local JAG office to ensure you are armed with the current facts regarding repossessions.*

- Service members (National Guard and Reserves) are also guaranteed Job Reinstatement once they return from active duty. If they meet the following conditions:

THE MILITARY SPOUSE

- Go to www.ESGR.org: What is Employer Support for the Guard and Reserve? Employer Support for the Guard and Reserve (ESGR) is a Department of Defense organization. It is a staff group within the Office of the Assistant Secretary of Defense for Reserve Affairs (ASD/RA), which is in itself a part of the Office of the Secretary of Defense.

- Here are some suggestions with regard to preparing to deploy or be mobilized:
    - Consult with your employer.
    - Keep them informed.
    - Make them feel like they are a part of the process.
    - Get all agreements in writing so that there can be no misunderstanding. Explain it is for your peace of mind and the protection of the company.
    - Before signing an agreement know your rights under the law.
    - Have the agreement reviewed by a JAG lawyer at your nearest base. If you are not close to a base, then get the number to the closest JAG office and call and ask to speak with a lawyer over the phone.

- Give the employer notice, before taking leave and let them know the leave is for military service.

- Spend no more than five years on leave for military service (there are exceptions to the five year rule in which the Service Member can serve longer provided certain conditions are met).

- Your release from military service is under honorable conditions.

- o Report back or apply for reinstatement within specified time limits (limits vary and may require research).

- o Employers are required by law to reinstate workers to the same position they would have held had they been continuously employed throughout their leave and provided they are otherwise qualified for that job. The employer must give you any promotions, increased pay, or additional job responsibilities that you would have received if you had not taken leave.

- o In addition, returning military members cannot be fired without cause for up to one year after being reinstated.

Since we, the authors, are not lawyers or experts in this area…**You must contact your legal office in your area to obtain the proper advice for your situation.** This information is provided only for information/education purposes. Laws do change and you may be entitled to more or less depending on your status and current law.

Ways To Save Your Money and Set up Your Family for Success:

- **If you are fortunate enough to have two incomes in your family:** Live off of one income (preferably the military members pay), and use the spouses pay as a method to save money. As military spouses, we tend to change jobs frequently. So if you pay the bills on the service members pay and save the spouse's pay, you will be financially stable and you will be able to absorb a period of unemployment and able to invest more. If you cannot currently live off of one income, we propose that you come up with a budget that allows you to utilize the second income to pay off your debts and begin saving/investing.

- **Pay yourself first:** Make yourself the first bill you decide to pay. We originally began saving $25 a month by buying a savings bond. Eventually we would increase that amount to $50 a month.

Twenty years later we were able to utilize this money for a down payment on our first home. However, if you decide to begin a savings plan, begin with an amount of money you can afford and stick to it no matter what. We preferred to put our money in a bank that we did not have immediate access to. This made us ask ourselves a question: Do we really want this or can it wait? Here are two examples of how we used this to our advantage. First we used payroll deduction for bonds. Second, we opened a savings account out of state (not readily accessible) and we did not have a debit or ATM card attached to it. This forced us to save and think before we used the money...this helps prevent impulse buying and helps develop financial discipline.

- On a daily basis empty your change into a container and save it. We have saved in excess of $1000 in a year by doing this.

- Start an automatic payroll deduction to a savings account, IRA, money market account or other savings vehicle. When you don't see the money....you don't miss it!

- **Once you have set aside a specific amount of money, try this technique:** Every year a service member will receive a *Cost of Living Raise,* usually between 2-4%. Check the Leave and Earnings Statement (LES) and determine how much the salary increased after taxes and save this amount of money. In addition, every two years, a service member receives a longevity raise along with the annual cost of living raise. Use the same rule in these cases. Since you lived without the money thus far...why spend it? Why not save it? Invest it, save it, or start a ROTH IRA account for you and your spouse. My husband and I applied this principle from the time he was a Sergeant (E-5) until he was promoted to Sergeant First Class (E-7) before we gave ourselves an increase in our budget. We went from saving $25 a month out of his pay to saving about $500 a month, all because we applied this principle. It gave us a great nest egg for emergencies and unforeseen events. In addition, we saved all my income. We invested some and saved part of it for vacations. You may also use this principle when a service member is promoted.

- **Paying off debts to save money and prepare for future purchases:** We found this method most useful. For example, when we paid off our first car, we continued to allow the money to go to the designated savings account. We had lived without this money for 3 years and were able to survive. By banking the car payment for another 4 years we were able to put a large down payment on our next car with a significant decrease in car payments. The bottom-line is this: once a bill is paid off, save that money and use it for investments or a future down payment on your next big ticket item. **This is an incredible savings tool!**

- **Don't pay with plastic:** Avoid paying with your credit card if you can, or place the charge on your credit card and pay it off when the bill comes due. It is too easy to play now and pay big later! It is important to establish and maintain your credit but do so in moderation. The best way to utilize the credit card is to only purchase what you have cash to pay for. **Save** for big ticket items! Use the credit in an emergency only and then only as a last resort. If you have to use a credit card in an emergency adjust your budget for a month or two and pay off the debt.

- **Buying furniture:** Furniture is typically marked up about 300%. Wait for it to go on sale, or it becomes last years model, or if it is seasonal furniture wait for the season to end. Ask for military discounts. Ask for a discount by buying a floor model. Never pay the asking price! We recently purchased a $1500 chair for $400. We purchased a floor model, got a discount, and then when we got the furniture home we realized the underside was torn and the merchant took off another $250.

- **Buying clothes:** Mangers have the ability to mark down items, even in big department stores, look for slightly soiled garments, or a garment missing a button, or mismatched seams.

THE MILITARY SPOUSE

- When buying items always ask "Is this the best price you can give me? Is it possible to get free or reduced delivery charges on large ticket items like furniture or appliances?"

- **Books:** Utilize the post library or even the public library. Many allow you to exchange paperback books. Drop one off and pick one up for free. Consider buying used books. They are cheaper and usually in good condition. Consider websites like Amazon.com but *beware of shipping charges.* Post or Installation libraries also have books on tapes or CDs for long trips. Another good website for books is www.fetchbook.info

Thrift Stores: On post thrift stores or the Salvation Army usually have good deals on clothing and other household items.

How To Read The Leave And Earnings Statement: Google the following article on the internet: *Understanding Your LES.* It will provide you detailed information on how to read and understand the leave and earnings statement. Know what you're getting paid, why you are receiving it, what you should be getting paid, and if you are getting paid for something you are not entitled. Remember the government will take their overpayment money back; and generally all at once *and without warning*. That means if you do not stop unauthorized pay quickly you could get paid $0.00 the next month depending on how much you owe the government. If you find you are being overpaid put the over payment aside to help you during the period when the government takes the money back to correct the overpayment. ***This is critical...do not spend this money like it is extra cash! It's not!*** If you owe the government a large sum of money you can usually request to have the money repaid over 12 months to reduce the burden of paying it back all at once...but only use this option if you have to. You must request this because they will not generally offer it to you.

How To Get A Leave And Earnings Statement: Currently, the Leave and Earning Statements are sent electronically either once or twice a month depending on how the service member chooses to be paid. The service member may choose to provide you with their pin number and you can check the LES while they are deployed or TDY.

Deployments: If you are deploying, try to set up all your bills by allotment or bank draft. It can reduce a lot of stress and it will ensure all your bills are paid on time as long as you have the money in your account to cover the bills.

Taxes, And How To Reduce Your Cost:

- **Filing taxes on post:** The military provides a service that will prepare your taxes for free and e-file them for you **at no charge** *(some special restrictions may apply...i.e. they may not file complex returns, business returns, and Reserve and National Guard soldier may be required to be activated for a specific period of time. Check with your local Post Tax Office. A good point of contact is normally the JAG office).* This is a significant savings for the service member. As tax season approaches watch for advertisements for the installation tax office. In addition, we would offer a word of caution about establishments off post that will lend you money on your income tax refund ahead of time for a small fee. This small fee is usually a large sum of money. It is often better to wait (e-file turn arounds do not take that long, I believe the IRS states 7 days...even if it takes 30 days you are better off to wait). If you cannot wait it is easier (and usually cheaper) to utilize a credit card or a signature loan if you must have the money immediately. But you should repay these as soon as you receive your refund... ***bottom-line: it is best to wait for your refund and have your taxes done for free on post!***

- **Traditional Individual Retirement Account (IRA):** This IRA allows you to reduce your taxes now and pay taxes on the money as you withdraw it later in life. If you and your spouse are not eligible to participate in an employee-sponsored retirement plan, you can deduct the full amount of your traditional IRA contribution (currently up to $5,000 for individuals; $10,000 for married couples filing a joint return). If you are eligible (and every military member typically is) your traditional IRA contribution is deductible only if your adjusted gross income falls within the limits established by the IRS.

- **Thrift Savings Plan:** Utilize the military thrift savings plan. If you start with 1-3 % eventually work your way up and save as much as possible. This money is taken out in *pre tax* dollars which decreases the amount of taxes you pay each month and saves you money. No matter if you plan to stay in the service for 2-4 years or for a career, it is an opportunity you should utilize.

- **ROTH IRA:** The benefit of the ROTH IRA is that you can put money away now and it is not taxable when you retire. Currently you and your spouse can put away $5,000 each into a ROTH IRA account. Income limits apply ROTH IRAs.

- **Savings Bonds:** While not the most lucrative of investment tools they are reliable and secure. Many people will steer you away from bonds. I will tell you that my husband and I bought $50 and $100 savings bonds every month for almost ten years. We stopped buying them and kept them until they matured. As a result we utilized them to help us come up with the down payment on our retirement home. Since we were first time home buyers and the bonds where used to buy our home, the interest was tax free. While it was not the most lucrative rate of return it was safe and it is how we got started saving money after we established our emergency fund. In addition, you can get tools on the internet that allow you to enter your bond information and it will recalculate the value of your bonds every month. Simply use a search engine like GOOGLE and type in Savings Bond Calculator. The US Treasury Department also has a useful website with numerous calculators and helpful tools. *In addition, savings bonds may also be used to pay college tuition without paying taxes on the amount.*

- **Transit account:** If you have to commute to work consider funding a transit account. You can save up to $105 a month for the cost of commuting on public transportation and $200 a month for parking. In addition if you don't spend the money it can be rolled over to the next year. (Source: *Money Magazine*, Nov. 2005)

Debt Consolidation: In his book, *Financial Peace,* author Dave Ramsey states,"The first 3 letters of the word consolidation say it all: *It's a con."* The bottom-line is that taking out a loan to pay a loan makes no sense. It may help you in the short term but in the long term it will cost you more and take longer to pay off the debt. The best thing you can do is modify your behavior. Come up with a plan (a budget) and stick to it. Pay your bills off and control future spending. ***Do not buy into a debt consolidation plan!***

- **Before you hire a credit counselor:** (*The following information extracted from Money Magazine November 2005 issue*) Money Magazine states in part that you should try to go it alone at first because you can haggle with credit card companies as well as counselors do. You can state that you will switch credit card companies, and this could result in the company dropping your interest rate between 1-3 points.

- Promise to pay on time…follow through with your promise and they may drop it further. Use a debt calculator like the one on *money.com* to determine how much you need to pay to reach your debt-free goal.

- *Many counselors will provide free consultation…take their advice and leave* because their debt management program will probably cost you more money. Take their good ideas and use them to your advantage.

Bankruptcy: In some cases service members may have to file bankruptcy. *Filing this action can have an adverse effect on a soldier's security clearance. Prior to filing bankruptcy we highly recommend you* *consult with ACS, legal, and a professional.* Do not take this action lightly. For some service members this may be their only possibility to get a fresh start. After seeking the proper advice, if you choose this route, make smart choices from this point forward in your life because a bankruptcy will have significant effects on your life and your families' life for at least 7 years and may stay on your credit reports for up to 10 years. Prior to filing for bankruptcy check to see exactly what the current laws are and the potential impact bankruptcy will have on your life. In addition, new bankruptcy laws (2005) were recently enacted making it tougher for individuals to file bankruptcy for credit card debt.

Disable Vets and "Fast Track" Chapter 7 Bankruptcy: Disabled veterans who incurred debt while on active duty may qualify to fast track Chapter 7 filings. This is part of the National Guard and Reservists Debt Relief Act of 2008. You must meet a two part test to qualify. The debtor must be rated by the Department of Veteran Affairs as 30 percent or more disabled and the debt must have occurred while on active duty.

Divorces: Today unfortunately divorces are on the rise. If possible consider minimizing your legal fees. It has been estimated that you can save as much as 65% of legal cost by cooperating with each other in a divorce. In addition, when it comes to big assets like homes it is usually better to sell them and split the profit rather than try to hang on to them with reduced incomes. Remember that the way you structure alimony or child support could have adverse consequences. **Alimony is taxable** for the individual receiving it and a tax deduction for the person providing it. Also consider how to split up other long term assets like retirement funds, college for the children, insurance policies, and ***don't forget to change/update beneficiaries on retirement plans, bonds, and insurance policies, wills, childcare, and next of kin notification.*** There are several books available to help you work through many of the issues. It is our sincere hope you do not have to apply any of these tools All marriages go through hard times and it is best emotionally and financially to try and find a way to work problems out together for the greater benefit of not just you and your spouse, but most importantly, for your children. If the marriage problems are related to deployments, contact

MilitaryOneSource.com to get free counseling which is *not* reported to your chain of command.

Credit Scores: *Usually, you must pay for a credit score report.* We suggest you read the November 2005 edition of Money Magazine for a more in-depth discussion. There are also several good books on how to improve your credit score. Most people believe that if their income goes up so does their credit score. That is not true! The fact is that credit scores reflect only your past credit history and not your income, martial status, occupation, or other personal characteristics. Most people believe that a married couple has a combined credit score. This is an incorrect assumption. Jointly owned debt can affect your individual credit score. To obtain a free brochure on understanding your credit score go to www.pueblo.gsa.gov. and click on the link for "money link". FICO credit scores range from 300-850. A score above 700 means you are relatively a low risk and will likely qualify for the best interest rate. Scores below 600 mean higher loan rates but may also mean that you could be denied insurance, telephone service, a job, or even an apartment. Each of the three major credit bureaus maintain a credit score on you. The credit bureaus are: Equifax, Tans Union, and Experian. Three different companies means you could have three different scores. **The two most important factors in determining your credit score are your payment history and how much you owe.** The fastest way to improve your credit score is to pay bills promptly and keep your credit card balances low. Do you want a better score? Then pay off debt rather than moving it from one credit card to another. Also keep in mind the following facts:

- Having only a few credit cards can hurt your credit score. This is because having a small credit profile means that a company cannot make a good assessment of how you pay your bills. You should consider opening another credit account or taking out an installment loan like a car loan. However, do not have more than 4 credit cards.

THE MILITARY SPOUSE

- Every time you request a credit card the issuers runs a credit report and the more inquires in a short period of time reduces your credit score.

- In the best case your balance on credit cards should not exceed 30% of the maximum you can charge….even if you routinely pay your bill in full it can look like you are spending too much in credit if you exceed the 30% range.

- If you consolidate your debts on to a low rate card and close the high rate credit card this can also be looked at in a negative manner and cause your credit score to drop. You could take two approaches to help your credit score. You could take out a low interest rate installment loan and pay of the high interest rate card, or transfer the debt to the lower interest rate card and do not close the higher interest rate card right away.

- Never throw away a credit card or any receipts with your account number on them. Cards and account numbers can be stolen. Cut up the cards and receipts, or better yet shred them.

- If you have always been on time with your bills and miss one payment because of an emergency or unforeseen event, your credit score will drop if your payment is late 30 days or more.

- To make the best of your credit score have 2-4 credit cards, at least 6 months old and a bank or installment loan.

- Understand that there is such a thing as "good debt" like a mortgage or car payment. Likewise, you can have "bad debt"
    - by not paying your bills on time,
    - or having a large amount of available credit

Other Sources Of Income/Off Duty Employment:

- **In home childcare:** At times it is difficult for spouses to get a job in some locations, especially overseas. Childcare in your home is an option if you and your spouse have the temperament for this type of business. You must undergo certain training and background checks and the financial and personal rewards are usually good. **Each service, base or installation has its own regulation or unique policies concerning home child care. Ensure you check with Army Community Service or our sister services equivalent agency. Home childcare on a military base is strictly regulated. In almost all other situations home businesses are not authorized to be run out of government quarters.**

- **Night jobs:** In some cases it is impractical for a spouse to work because the jobs do not pay enough to pay for childcare, taxes, and leave enough to make working worthwhile. In these situations it may be better for you or your spouse to consider getting an evening or weekend job. The military requires service members to receive approval from the Commander for off duty employment. With increased security, delivery businesses are looking for individuals with military ID cards so that they can deliver products such as fast food on post. Ensure you balance night jobs or off duty employment with your family time. You have to strike a balance between work and family.

Emergency Fund: As we discussed earlier, pay yourself first! Before you begin to invest, establish an emergency fund of between 1-3 months pay. This provides you the latitude to handle unforeseen expenses and still allows you the ability to continue to save.

The Act Of Giving (Reciprocity): Before we begin to talk about investing in our futures, I would like to take a moment to talk about giving to others that are less fortunate than ourselves. The spirit of giving without the expectation of return is a great trait and if all of us give a little we can make a huge difference in this world. You may choose to give by: supporting a church or other non-profit organizations (which is tax deductible) with a monetary gift, giving money to better the life of another person (on an individual basis which is not normally tax deductible), giving your time to charities, giving items to a needy family. Either way, giving is a positive attribute when done with a willing and sincere desire to help someone less fortunate than ourselves.

- One method we practice in our home (aside from normal tithe) is 1-2 times a year we ask our daughter to sit down and go through her clothes and toys. We ask her to set aside things that she no longer plays with or wears and ask that she set them aside to be given to another child less fortunate or to an organization dedicated to helping children. Needless to say, the first few times this was a traumatic event in her life....you would have thought the world was going to end. It is only when we give of ourselves that we can truly appreciate the blessings we have received in our own lives. Our family truly believes that what you give out of pureness of heart comes back to you tenfold.

- We ask that you consider not only giving things to others less fortunate but also that you give time to your community. By giving you will receive much in return. The return ranges from a kind word of thank you to a potential larger blessing you never expected. Again, give not to get but to make another's life more tolerable and to provide others an opportunity. $10 in an envelope given anonymously to a few needy families is a great holiday tradition as well. You will be surprised with the blessings you receive!

Investing: Once you have a handle on your debt, are sticking to a budget and have established an emergency fund, it is time to start looking at investing. There are several agencies that normally deal with military members which can provide financial services with regard to investing, insurance, banking, and various other services. The two most prominent are First Command Financial Planning and USAA. **We are not endorsing these companies simply making you aware of them.** They typically cater to military families. The **key is to find an agent that is honest and has your best interest at heart.** Remember that these individuals are in business to make money. One of the ways they make money is to sell insurance. There is a level of insurance everyone needs and you must determine for yourself what that level is. Never feel pressured to make a decision. If you feel pressured odds are your dealing with the wrong agent. *Do not give up, just find another agent.*

- **Powers of Attorney and Financial Transactions:** Powers of Attorney generally come in two forms: General Power of Attorney, and Special Power of Attorney. A **General Power of Attorney** basically authorizes another person to do anything in your absence just as if you were present. For example: buy a home, a new car, liquidate any financial savings or investments. A **Special Power of Attorney** limits the ability of the person you authorize to act only in a specific manner or circumstance. For example: you could give an individual a Special Power of Attorney to register your car or to sell your car. **However, it is worthy to note that many financial institutions and real estate agents/lawyers may not accept a General Power of Attorney**. Some may honor the General Power of Attorney if it is less than 6 months old, others may want a Special Power of Attorney. It is imperative that you check with all your financial institutions to see what their policies are when implementing a power of attorney. These policies are designed to protect the service member and their family. *JAG can provide you with either one.*

- **Mutual Funds:** These come in all shapes and sizes. They range from sector funds to broad based funds. You can usually buy funds two ways:
    - **Loaded Fund:** Comes with an upfront sales charge, meaning that anytime you invest the company charges you

a fee ranging form 3% to 5.75%. The cost of a loaded fund is to pay the financial planner that assists you with your decisions. If you are going to do everything yourself, do not use this type of fund. If you are going to use an advisor, the sales charge is how they get paid to help you. No matter what you do try to invest money every month no matter what. (This practice is also known as dollar cost averaging). There is no evidence to suggest that a loaded fund performs better than a no load fund. Some funds are marketed as no load funds but have a CDSC (Contingent Deferred Sales Charge) or back-end load. This means they charge you a fee to withdraw your money in the first few years of owning it. Ensure you know what the charges are before you invest.

- **No Load Fund:** True no load funds do not charge you a sales charge to invest your money. These funds are designed for the do-it-yourself-er, since you are not paying for and do not get help. There is nothing wrong with this approach *if* you really know what you are doing. You are responsible for making all the decisions with regard to investing. You will have to do all the paperwork over the phone/internet and through the mail and research each fund completely and frequently.

The best advice we can give about mutual funds is to do your research. Check with several large investment companies like Fidelity, Vanguard, Janus, etc. and review the funds they offer. Talk to different financial planning firms. Carefully read the literature on the funds and what the administrative fees are along with the sales charges. We would also encourage you to read books on mutual funds such as *Mutual Funds for Dummies*. Some funds will allow you to invest as little as $50 a month. This is great for young couples just starting off. ***Do your homework* and know exactly what you are getting into.**

TIP: A government allotment which takes the money out before you see it is a painless way to invest regularly.

- **Dividend Reinvestment Plans (DRIPS):** Nearly 1,000 publicly traded companies now offer DRIPS. DRIPS allow you to buy fractional shares of a company by investing as little as $10. The best plans give you a discount of 3-5% when buy shares this way. An excellent way to learn about DRIPS is to visit the DRIPS investor. See the website chapter in this book for their web address. In addition, you can also visit company websites like Home Depot and Disney. They offer DRIPS plans.

- **Spouse Retirement Fund:** If your spouse has a retirement fund such as a 401(K) or a profit sharing plan encourage them to fully invest in it. Or at least invest to the amount that you can afford. Find out if the company will match any contributions (put their money in to help your money grow). Be careful to **ensure that your spouse does not solely invest** in company stock that he or she may work for. This can be dangerous. Ensure your money is diversified through several investments. Never put all your eggs in one company stock. Recent years have seen numerous examples of individuals who only had shares of company stock and watched the company go bankrupt and the workers' hopes and dreams of retirement went down with the company.

- **Certificates Of Deposit (CDs):** Are another vehicle for earning interest. They are usually guaranteed and safe but have a lower rate of return (or interest rate).

- **Money Market Funds:** These typically give higher yields than CDs however their safety is not normally guaranteed and it is possible to lose the money invested in these instruments.

- **Online Investing:** Is another option available to a service member's family. This is a risky adventure and not for the faint of heart. My husband and I have had some success with this type of

THE MILITARY SPOUSE

investment but we understand it is dangerous and risky. It is not for the beginning investor. I like to call it "legalized gambling"... because everyday you play the stock market you are taking a chance. If you choose to utilize this method, I would offer the following advice: read about it, and invest what you can afford to lose. I suggest reading *Investing Online for Dummies* and also *Stock Investing for Dummies*. I would also encourage you only to invest an amount of money that you can reasonably afford to lose without endangering your family or your financial security. *This method also requires constant research to stay current.*

Identity Theft - It Can Happen To You: Identity Theft is a crime that continues to grow and you should take steps to help prevent the theft of your identity.

- **How does someone steal your identity?** By using your name, personal information like driver's license, telephone number, investment accounts or bank account numbers, social security number, credit card numbers. Not only can they open new accounts, but in some cases it may be possible to gain access to your existing accounts.

Tips To Protect Your Identity: Here are a few tips on how to guard your identity and how to take action should you believe you are a victim of identity theft:

- Don't give out your social security number: *some establishments will require this information in order to provide services. These may include:* financial institutions, medical companies (for insurance purposes), military offices often do business utilizing your social. **The bottom line:** Don't just provide the information casually; ask why it is needed. If you are suspicious don't provide it until you are positive you need to provide it.

- Before giving out any personal information such as birth date, maiden name, address or other items mentioned above, find out why it is required and how it will be used.

- Consider putting a 7 year permanent fraud alert in place with all 3 major credit reporting firms.

- Protect the social security numbers of all family members. When individuals ask to verify your social security numbers, see if they will accept another way of verifying your information. If not, ask to speak with a manager.

- Shred any information that contains your personal information. Don't just tear it up. Invest in a paper shredding machine that cross shreds so that information cannot be read once the paper is passed thru the shredder.

- Mail: drop your mail off at a secure location like a post office or locked mail box. Remove incoming mail promptly or utilize a mail box with a locking system, if possible. Contact your post office and request your mail be stopped during prolonged absences from home, or have a trustworthy person collect your mail daily.

- Do not keep critical paperwork such as birth certificates, passports, social security cards on your person or in areas that are easily accessible.

- When using computers, create passwords that have nothing to do with you, your family, or your job. Make it something unique and creative that someone cannot easily identify it with you. Try never to write down user IDs and passwords.

TIP: On the back of all Credit/Debit Cards write the words "SEE ID". ***Do not sign them!*** *This requires a sales person or cashier to ask for positive identification in order to confirm you are the person entitled to utilize the card!*

THE MILITARY SPOUSE

- Place different passwords on all your accounts for example: credit cards, phone, banks, etc.

- Annually get a copy of your credit report from the major credit reporting agencies.

- Keep a list of the sensitive items you have in your wallet or purse: credit cards, insurance cards, driver's license, bank account cards, identification cards for work or military identification, account cards used at local stores to enter or purchase items (book stores, wholesale clubs...etc).

TIP: A good method is to use a copy machine and place several items on the machine and copy them. By doing this you have a copy of your sensitive items.

- Always secure personal information in a secure location in your home, preferably out of sight and in a secure container not easily accessible. ***Make sure it is stored in a fire proof container.*** It would also be wise to make two copies and store them in separate locations.

- Never carry your social security card with you and or your personal access numbers to your bank accounts or debit/credit cards.

- Check all your account statements when they come in. Look for any suspicious purchases or any debts you cannot account for or did not authorize. Call the company to question any suspicious transactions.

- Utilize a good "Firewall" on your computer that protects personal data, blocks cookies, and other spyware. Do not store personal information on your computer.

- **When traveling, shopping or away from home:**

    o Whenever you use a credit card or debit card watch for individuals looking over your shoulder. Cover the key pad as you make your entries. Individuals have been known to watch from a distance with binoculars or other devices to gather credit card number (for example, when you utilize a public phone). *Never hold your credit card or leave it on a restaurant table with the numbers facing up.*

    o Utilize cash purchases sparingly especially during the holiday season. Individuals have been known to watch people purchase items, follow them, steal the items with the receipt and then return them for cash. *Do not hesitate to ask mall or store security personnel to escort you to your car after dark. In addition keep all the items you purchase in the trunk of your car so that they cannot be seen.*

    o Checks: Use these only when necessary. Individuals can obtain enough information about you on your check to possibly steal your identity. Do not have your phone number or social security number pre-printed on your checks. Our recommendation is only utilize them when you have to. In addition, if you utilize credit cards, normally you are only responsible by law for the $50 of unauthorized use; however, the loss must be reported immediately. In addition, credit cards contain far less personal information than checks.

    o Never leave your purse or wallet in an open area, even at work. Keep only the essential items in your wallet or purse. Lock them up if at all possible. Only carry the credit cards you will use that day. This helps reduce your potential loss.

THE MILITARY SPOUSE

- o When traveling, if at all possible, use a cell phone or a prepaid calling card. This prevents possible theft of your credit card information.

- **Solicitation:**

    - o If you did not initiate the contact (for example, a phone call) ask for the name of the individual you are speaking with, the company they represent, and a call back number. Find out how they received your name. To reduce unwanted solicitation, sign yourself up for the National Do Not Call list at www.donotcall.gov.

    - o Use Caller ID to screen unwanted calls.

    - o Never provide personal information over the phone, thru mail, or the internet unless you are absolutely positive that the transaction is legitimate. If you have a question when utilizing your information online call your financial institution and speak with the fraud department.

    - o If you would like to give money to an organization it is recommended that you make contact with that organization directly by utilizing local calling numbers. Do not accept solicitation or request for charity and personal information unless you initiated contact.

    - o Before returning calls try to verify who the number actually belongs to. The goal is to know who you are calling to reduce your exposure to possible con artists or scams.

- **What should I do if I suspect my identity has been stolen?**

    - o File a police report on the incident or incidents.

- Contact the financial institution immediately.

- Immediately contact all credit card companies, banks or other financial institutions in writing (utilizing return receipt) or by emailing (a specific person and also "cc" or carbon copy yourself on the email you send).

- Maintain a file of all information pertaining to the incident: who you contacted, when you spoke with them, the agency they work for, time and date, also consider following up in writing.

- Close the account.

- Contact the institution in which the purchase was made.

- Notify financial institutions that you utilize that any new request for credit cards, loans or other financial accounts must be approved by you personally by either phone contact or in person.

- Immediately request credit reports from all three major credit reporting agencies. These are free when you are a victim of identity theft.

- Know when your bills and new credit cards will usually arrive. If they don't arrive on time call the financial or other institution to see if they are late and if they have been mailed out. Make sure the bills are going to the correct address.

- Request a "fraud alert" on all your accounts.

- Contact the Federal Trade Commission: www.ftc.gov/bcp/edu/microsites/idtheft/. They provide and maintain a database of identity theft cases and provide useful information to victims.

- **How do I protect my Social Security Number?**

    o If you are conducting business online, ensure the site is secure. Do not pass personal information in casual emails. When shopping online the icon of a lock at the bottom of a screen indicates a secure site. Only buy from websites that you trust.

    o Check Privacy Act information in all agreements you enter to ensure your information will not be shared or if you can opt out of your information being shared. Do not sign or enter into an agreement or transaction without reading it.

    o If you are asked for your social security number find out why and for what purpose the information will be utilized.

    o ***Do not:***
      - Make your driver's license number the same as your Social Security Number.
      - Carry your Social Security Card with you.
      - Place your Social Security Number on your checks.

- **Who has the right to demand your Social Security Number?**
  All businesses can ask for your Social Security Number, but that does not mean you have to provide it. Ask if they will accept another form of identification. If not, perhaps you do not want to do business with them...and more than likely they won't want to do business with you. Here is list of some organizations that will require your social security number:

    o Motor Vehicle Department.

    o Welfare Departments.

- o Financial Institutions required for reporting tax information.
- o Tax Departments.

- **How to get off mass mailing lists:**

  - o Contact companies directly and ask them to take you off their mailing lists.

  - o Email is an excellent method for sending such a request.

  - o You may also get your name taken off many lists by contacting several agencies. They are:

    <u>**For National Direct Mail Lists:**</u> go to www.the–dma.org or write to them at: DMA, Mail Preference Service, P.O. Box 9008, Farmingdale, NY 11735.

    <u>**For Telephone Marketers:**</u> go to www.the-dma.org or write them at DMA Telephone Preference Service P.O. Box 9014, Farmingdale, NY 11735.

    <u>**For Telephone Marketers:**</u> go to www.donotcall.gov.

    <u>**For Credit Cards**</u>: call 1-888-567-8688.

    <u>**For Email Direct Mailing Lists**</u>: got to http://www.dmaconsumers.org/consumerassistance.html

- **How to get a copy of your credit reports:** It is wise to order a copy of your credit reports from all three agencies at least once a year. You can obtain one free copy a year from each agency, otherwise there is normally a charge associated with a request. Don't become a victim of Identity Theft!

THE MILITARY SPOUSE

- Trans Union: 800-888-4213 or www.tuc.com to report Fraud: 800-680-7289.

- Experian: 888 397-3742 or www.experian.com to report Fraud: 888-397-3742.

- Equifax: 800-685-1111 or www.equifax.com to report Fraud: 800-525-6285.

- **What else could I do if I suspect my information has been or may have been compromised?**

  - Contact one of the credit agencies listed above and they usually offer a program for a fee, and this program allows you to monitor your accounts, be alerted of suspicious activity, and receive free credit reports.

- **How do I get free credit reports?**

  - By law you can receive one free credit report from each reporting agency listed above. Simply go to *www.ftc.gov/freereports* and request your annual free report.

  - **Note:** *If you are a victim of identity theft all credit reports are free!*

- **Spouse Unemployment resulting from Permanent Change of Station (PCS):**
  - 27 states currently offer unemployment benefits for Spouses that must give up their jobs as a result of Permanent Change of Station (PCS) Moves.
  - Check with your local unemployment office concerning your qualification and the state laws specific to the state involved.

PATRICIA GERECHT & MARK GERECHT

CHAPTER 3
OUR CHILDREN AND MONEY

Teaching Your Children To Save: Saving habits are best taught when children are young. Here are several suggestions:

- **Giving more than we can afford:** At times we may give our children more than we can afford. This is an area that may need your attention. If you control your spending correctly it can educate your children and save the family money. Remember you cannot purchase love…and love cannot be measured by material things.

- **The latest and greatest:** Talk with your children and explain that it is not necessary to have the latest and greatest… that buying things does not equate to love. It is better to give children a budget and have them save money and earn privileges than to have them continuously expect material gifts from you.

- **Helping them build a future:** It is important to let our children know that we are building a future for them by saving now.

- **Model behavior:** Teach them the value of avoiding impulse buying by modeling it. We are not saying don't buy for your children… we are saying buy in moderation. Set the example for them and let them learn the importance of earning something. Buying our children unneeded items can account for a large sum of monthly income.

- **Chores:** Develop a list of things for your child to do around the house. Then be clear that they will receive earnings for each task. If the child completes the task to the pre-determined standard, they are paid in the form of a weekly allowance. Should the child fail to do the task, the amount is deducted from the allowance. In effect, the child could make nothing for substandard performance.

- **The "½ Method":** Another method is to offer to pay ½ of the price of an item if your child will pay the other ½.

- **Charity, save, spend:** Have your child break their money into 3 envelopes. 1 for spending, 1 for savings, and 1 for charity or giving. They can give to another child, church or any worthwhile organization designed to help the community. This process teaches children how to save for something they want, provides money for things they want now, and most importantly teaches them to think of others less fortunate than themselves. As the money grows it can be transferred to a bank account.

- **Encourage education:** We utilize educational benefits in our home. For example: at the age of about 3 ½ our daughter was told that when she could count to 100 by ones she would receive a 1 dollar bill. The bill had to be broken up into 10% for charity, 30% for spending, and 60% for savings. We continued to set goals like this such as counting to 100 by fives, then by tens, and then when she could complete all her adding flash cards she received additional money. We found this to be an exceptional motivator for our child. She was proud of what she accomplished and we were proud to see her succeed. You may also want to consider paying your child for obtaining good grades in school. Set an amount for an "A", so much for a "B" and so much for a "C". The idea is to pay more for an "A" than a "C" and to pay nothing for a grade below a "C". *Every day our children go to school like we go to work. Show them you are paid on results and pay them for their grades when their report cards come out.*

- **"401P (Parent Fund)":** As your child gets older and begins to really understand money and how it works (how a bank account works) I would encourage you to consider implementing something we call the 401P (parent fund). This means that for

THE MILITARY SPOUSE

every dollar our child gives us for savings we will match it and invest it in a bank account, mutual fund, or other savings instrument. *Some children catch onto this very quickly and realize that this is an immediate 100% return on investment.* Therefore depending on how many children you have or how determined your child is, you may have to establish a cap on matching funds. This is a great way to focus children, build financial discipline, and most of all teach them to think of others before they think of themselves. If your child has reportable (W-2) income, consider putting the 401P funds into a Roth IRA for them. There are mutual funds that allow minors to open these accounts with a parent's signature.

- **Brand names:** Teach your children that fashion statements can ruin their financial situation. When they want you to buy those designer jeans for $80 rather than the $20 pair, ask them to use their money rather than feeling free to spend your money. Or offer to pay for them and they can pay you back on a weekly basis using their allowance, **but you must stick to this and make them pay you back at a realistic rate. This makes them learn about impulse buying, buying on credit (your money), and enforces financial discipline**. Do they really need that new electronic gadget or computer game…or can they wait a few weeks and buy it used on an auction site or used at a computer store for less or maybe even half the price? They will quickly realize their money doesn't go as far as they think it does.

- Explain monetary issues to your children in terms they can understand. For example: your child may want a new computer game. If you tell them you will purchase the game for them but it will equate to 6 hours of work to pay you back for the purchase. Perhaps you could tie the amount of money per hour to the minimum wage.

- Have you ever had the experience of taking your child into a store and he or she picks something up and it breaks (remember "If you

53

break it you bought it")? Here is a method that might help: Depending on the age of your child give them an amount of money (a quarter, a dollar, etc.) and tell them if they keep their hands in their pockets the whole time they are in the store or stores for the entire trip they get to keep the money. If they remove their hands they have to give the money back to you. This is a good teaching tool in terms of self discipline, following instructions, and it might just save you from paying for a very expensive piece of merchandise.

- As your children get older introduce them to savings accounts, checking accounts and credit cards. Teach them how to manage their money and credit. Teaching these skills early in life will pay big dividends in the future. To teach financial responsibility early it may be a good idea to provide your child with an emergency credit card in case their car breaks down or they experience some other unforeseen emergency. This may help you gauge how financially responsible your children are.

A child that understands the power of saving money for the future, maintaining money for daily activity, and the power of helping others will be a child you can trust to do the right thing not only while you are there but while you are away. This process builds self esteem, trust, and instills in children, at a young age, the importance of giving of themselves to help others.

CHAPTER 4
BUYING A HOME

Things You Should Know Before You Buy A Home: This portion will be dedicated to simply providing some insight into the process of home buying. It is best to do research on your own and check out everything involved in the process. Don't just take a real estate agent's word or the builder's word. After all, they make a living by selling houses, not homes. Make an informed decision...no one protects your interests better than you.

- **Things to know before you buy**:

    o Know what you want in a house.

    o What you **DO NOT** want in a house?

    o Do you want to build?

    o Do you want to buy an existing home? New or pre-owned?

    o What are the most important aspects of the home?

    o Do some research on the web. Typically the farther you get from the city the cheaper the houses and the property.

    o Research the schools, check the chamber of commerce website and look to see how the schools compare with the national average, or if they are over crowded.

    o Do a web search and look for convicted child abuse offenders.

- o Know what you can afford. Get pre-approved for a loan before you begin house hunting.

- o Buy a book on home buying.

- o Before you begin this adventure know what to expect, because your level of understanding will determine how well you can protect yourself from overcharged services.

- **What type of mortgage should you get - fixed or variable?** A fixed rate provides you peace of mind and a stable payment. A variable rate could end up costing you more than you expect. Variable rates may be good for individuals who only plan to stay in a home for 3-10 years. But you must also consider the fact that interest rates may go up and increase your mortgage payment

- **20% down payment:** It's best to have a 20% down payment, because this prevents you from paying Private Mortgage Insurance (PMI). If you cannot afford a 20% down payment ensure you keep track of the equity in your home. When it reaches 20% you may be eligible to have the PMI removed from your mortgage payment. If you choose a VA loan PMI is not necessary but you are required to pay a fee, but the fee is less than 20% and your interest rate is usually higher than with a regular loan, depending on your credit rating.

- **80/15/5 mortgage:** A fairly new type of mortgage - this means you make a 5% down payment, take out an 80% 1st mortgage (amortized over 15 or 30 years), and a 15% 2nd mortgage (usually amortized over 15 years at a 1-2% higher interest rate). You may pay more on a monthly basis, but will not need to come to the table with as much money as with a normal 20% down payment and you still avoid paying PMI. This is a good option for those who do not have or do not wish to use their cash for a down payment.

THE MILITARY SPOUSE

- **Get pre-approved:** Getting pre-approved for a loan makes the process a lot easier. This can give you leverage in bargaining and possibly even helps you get a better price when the seller knows you are serious and already approved.

- **How much house do you need?** A conservative rule of thumb is to try and limit your housing expenses to 3 times your gross annual salary. All the cost of the home: mortgage, taxes, insurance should not be more than 30% of your gross income. Do not guess at this amount, compute it.

- **House inspection:** Always have an independent housing inspection done. *A word of caution, do not accept an inspection from an inspector hired or recommended by the seller.* Look for a reputable individual. Ask around and get names. You want to know what you are getting (what condition is the house in?) and if there are any hidden problems with the home. *Ensure you get a termite inspection as well and that you have an up to date termite bond that includes repair and re-treatment clauses.* You may want any problems the inspector finds to be fixed before you buy, or you may wish to use this information as a negotiating tool in the selling price. In addition, some states are known as "buyer beware" states, meaning an owner does not have to disclose problems with the home. *Make sure you know if you live in one of these states!* **You may wish to find out when the inspector will check your home.** You can ask to accompany them during the inspection. If they do not agree, **find another inspector.**

- **How to prepay on your mortgage:** First, you need to make sure there is no penalty for paying off your mortgage early. In fact, we would highly encourage you to ensure your mortgage has no penalty for early pay off. Do this before signing the mortgage contract. Here are 2 easy ways to reduce the pay off of your home:

    o *Pay an additional payment each year*: Take your

monthly mortgage payment and divide it by 12. This is 1/12 of your mortgage. If you add this amount to your mortgage every month you will have made an additional payment each year and reduced the amount of interest paid. This will knock off about 5-7 years of your mortgage.

- *Make two payments a month*: Coordinate with your mortgage company to see if they will allow you to make payments twice a month, each for ½ the amount of the month mortgage payment. This will reduce the amount of interest you pay over the life of the loan.

- **Everything is negotiable:** When it comes to buying a home everything is negotiable. From commissions, how closing costs are paid, to who pays for housing inspections. You name it! A good rule of thumb is to treat others like you would like to be treated. Imagine yourself as the seller…how you would like to be treated by a perspective buyer.

- **If you are building a new home:**

    - Get everything in writing.

    - Stop by the home site on a regular basis. Workmen typically take short cuts (sometimes by accident and sometimes because they can).

    - Make sure you are getting what you paid for. In addition, ask for a clause that allows you to have a four phased independent inspection of the home. For example: reserve the right to have a foundation, framing, electric, and final inspection. This is a great tool if you believe your builder is not building to code. In addition, if a builder refuses this type of clause perhaps it is because there is a problem with the standards of the builder.

THE MILITARY SPOUSE

- Before you select a builder, drive through subdivisions they have built and talk to home owners to see if they are satisfied.

- Get to know the work crews on your house. Stop by and occasionally bring them something to drink or eat. Be friendly. They may do things for you on the job for a fraction of the price or may be willing to come back after closing to do something to the home for less than the builder would charge.

PATRICIA GERECHT & MARK GERECHT

CHAPTER 5
INSURANCE

Life Insurance: Only buy the amount of insurance you and your family need. When determining your needs make sure you plan for future needs as well. *Consider purchasing enough insurance to payoff major debts and provide a cushion for your family during the transition period.* There are insurance calculators on the market that can assist you in determining how much insurance you need. Again, **don't just look at your current needs…evaluate your future needs as well.** Will you be retiring soon? Is a child expected? Do you expect to buy a home and is there enough insurance to pay the house off if you suddenly die? *Most importantly, make sure that your insurance does not have a war clause or aviation clause. This means the policy will not pay if the death is a result of war or an aviation accident…make the insurance sales person show you this in writing…don't let him/her tell you about it…make him/her show it to you…absolutely no exceptions.*

Bottom line: you do not want to burden your family. You need enough insurance to take care of your needs and those of your family members. No matter how you slice it, life insurance is a fact and you will not escape it unless you choose to put your loved ones at risk. While in the military we become accustomed to great insurance at fairly cheap rates. Recently, the government even allowed spouses and children to be covered by insurance. The problem is that too many of us take the Service Members Group Life Insurance (SGLI) program for granted. As we begin to retire or separate from the military, we realize we cannot replace our military insurance for a cheap price. **Therefore, it is best to buy life insurance when we are young. The younger the better.** If we had to do it over again, our family would have bought substantially more life insurance on both of us when we were younger. Insurance doesn't get any cheaper as time goes on. Get what you can afford early in life because it only gets more expensive as you get older. If you, the military spouse, can get group life insurance where you work, take advantage of it. Think of this as a team venture and ensure you have adequate coverage on the spouse and service member. The military member will normally be the primary means of income, but what happens if something happens to the non military spouse? *The military member more than likely will continue to work but will need additional income to provide for childcare, possible relocation, or perhaps he/she may not be able to remain in the service.* Therefore, develop a plan that looks at the whole family.

Life Insurance for your children: You can purchase life insurance for your children, and in some cases it can be purchased while you are pregnant. We tend to believe it is a good idea to buy insurance for your children when they are young for several reasons: normally the premiums are low and most policies will guarantee insurability and coverage as your children age. (Check the policy for this clause.) This is important in the event your child later has some type of illness or injury that may affect future insurability.

Service Member Group Life Insurance (SGLI): If initially turned down, the military member may not be eligible to receive insurance under this program in the future or they may have to undergo a medical screening. Our advice is to take maximum benefit of the protection SGLI affords for the military member, spouse, and children. For the cost, you can't beat it!

Credit Life Insurance: In our personal opinion it is a waste of money. It is cheaper to buy term life insurance which will provide you more insurance for less money than to buy credit life insurance. Term life insurance is also portable and it can cover whatever you need it to cover. Credit life insurance only covers the one debt you purchased it for. Typically these products are offered when you purchase large ticket items such as a car or a home. We would strongly recommend that you factor this into your overall insurance plan rather than buy credit life. *Make sure that you review any loan paperwork carefully before you sign it. Many insurance agents will include credit life without asking for your permission. Remember it is not a requirement, it is your choice. They may also try to tell you something like, "Oh it's such a small amount of*

money and if provides great peace of mind in the event of a death"...
Remember term life covers everything, it is usually cheaper for more coverage, it can be used to pay off any debt, and you can spend it as you see fit.

Auto Insurance:

- *Don't buy minimum coverage.* When buying auto insurance the cheapest policy is not the best policy. Many states allow you to drive with only minimum coverage of say $15,000/$30,000. Most vehicles cost more than $15,000, add to that the fact that many accidents involve more than one vehicle and $15,000 is gone rather quickly. We strongly encourage you to take at a minimum $100,000/$300,000 coverage and more if you can afford it.

- ***Vendor Single Interest (VSI) Insurance:*** *Make sure you keep your auto and home owners insurance up to date:* VSI is a form of insurance that the lender buys in the event you let your insurance lapse. More simply put, VSI is coverage that protects the lender. In most cases the lender simply adds the cost of the insurance (which is usually at a higher rate than you could personally obtain the insurance on your own) into the remaining portion of your loan. *It is critically important you avoid VSI insurance. This may also have an impact on your credit rating.*

- *Do buy:*

    o **Underinsured motorist coverage:** (the cost is minimal). Should you be involved in an accident with a driver that is only carrying $15,000 worth of coverage your insurance company will pick up the remaining part of the bills up to the coverage you have.

    o **Uninsured motorist coverage:** (the cost is minimal). In the
    event you are hit by a driver who does not have insurance, you will be covered by this provision. Also take advantage

of rental insurance. If you vehicle cannot be driven your insurance company will pay for a rental car, usually, for a period of 14-30 days while your vehicle is being repaired.

- **Take a higher deductible:** Pick a deductible you can afford to pay. By picking a higher deductible you can dramatically reduce your monthly insurance premium.

- **Shop around**. We maintained insurance with a company for about 10 years. We thought loyalty meant something. We later switched companies and received a higher amount of coverage for a lower price. Our old insurance company continues to call wanting our business back....*imagine tha*t! Shop around every 2 years or so - you will be surprised at the difference. Make sure you are getting every discount available from "good driver", multiple car, multiple policy, seat belt, air bag, new car, good grade discount for students, military discount....ask the company what discounts they offer and if you are getting full credit for all discounts you are entitled to. In addition, see if taking a defensive driving course will reduce your premium.

Home or Renters Insurance: Basically the same principles apply to home and renters insurance. Remember that if there is a problem like a fire in your government quarters you will need renters insurance to replace your household items. If the government finds you at fault for the fire or other damage you could be held financially liable as well. Therefore, it is wise to seek the advice of a certified financial planner and an insurance agent you can trust.

- **Do:**
  - Get as much as you need to be able to rebuild the house and/or refurnish it. In addition check to see if your policy provides additional coverage at no charge. For example you may insure your home for $250,000 (the purchase price; and your policy may provide an additional 25%

above the purchase price in the event you need to rebuild. This allows for inflation, increased property value, etc. It is an excellent benefit to have.)

- o Shop around.

- o Take the highest deductible you can afford to pay. This can dramatically reduce your premium.

- o **Consider an umbrella policy for approximately one million dollars**. This policy protects you above anything that your auto and home owners/renters insurance does not. For example, if you are in an accident or if someone falls while on your property and you are held liable above and beyond the limits of your policy, the umbrella policy kicks in and covers the remainder of the judgment up to 1 million dollars. This helps to ensure those things that you have worked so hard for all your life cannot be taken away through a lawsuit. Usually insurance companies will require you to have both your home owners and auto insurance through them before they issue an umbrella policy.

- Ask about discounts:

    - o **Discounts:**
        - New home.
        - Military discounts.
        - Burglar alarms reduce your rate especially if they are monitored.
        - Monitored Fire Alarm systems.

Disability Insurance And Cancer Insurance: In addition to the insurance we have already discussed you may be eligible through your place of employment for disability, dismemberment insurance and cancer insurance. Depending on the cost of these insurance programs I would encourage you to check into them. They afford another level of protection that you should consider. You may not deem these as necessary because your spouse is on active duty, but there may come a time when you are no longer on active duty or a member of your family is in need of these types of services. Investigate your options before you turn them down. Understand that **usually** cancer insurance and disability insurance are paid to you directly and not a medical institution. *Consider family history and current habits in making your decision.*

Long Term Care Insurance: This insurance will provide protection in the event that you need in home or nursing home care in your senior years. It is usually not recommended to get this insurance until you reach on average the age of 50. Here is some information about long term care insurance:

- 48.6% of people over the age of 65 may spend time in a nursing home.

- About 10% of those 65 years of age will stay in care for 5 or more years.

- Four out of five couples will have at least one spouse in nursing home care.

- The number of people receiving in home care is rising each year. Some policies may cover this as well, so check before you buy.

- **Before you buy** you should know:

    o What the average cost of for in-home care and nursing home care is in your area.

    o How much of a benefit would you like to receive per day? For example, if care in your area is $170 per day you may wish to plan for care at $220 per day.

THE MILITARY SPOUSE

- o How long do you want your plan to cover you: 1 year, 2 years, or 3-5 years?

- o What is the maximum benefit you need from your policy?

- o How long do you wish to wait before your Long Term Care starts once you have problems? 30 days, 60 days, 90 days?

- o How much should your policy increase each year to keep up with inflation?

- o Do you wish your spouse to be covered by this plan?

- o What % will Medicare/Medicaid pay?

We are not insurance salesmen but think that the information contained in this chapter should be considered prior to making any decisions.

PATRICIA GERECHT & MARK GERECHT

THE MILITARY SPOUSE

CHAPTER 6
THE DO'S AND DON'TS OF SOCIAL GRACES FOR A MILITARY SPOUSE

Some spouses take on the military member's rank, either knowingly or unknowingly. Either way, it is not the best way to make friends or impress people. Never use your spouse's rank or position in conversation to obtain influence, personal gain, or gain the lime light. You don't wear your spouse's rank or position and you are not entitled to any special favors as a result of the service member's rank or position. <u>The only exception to this is for seating purposes at an official functions and this depends on who will be attending the function.</u> Here are some simple rules to go by that will be of tremendous help if you choose to follow them:

Note: If an item(s) has an * before it...**you won't find it in a formal protocol book!** It's either common sense *(treat people like you want to be treated)* or a down to earth approach. There are plenty of formally written protocol books out there, and while protocol is important, we believe in the basic principle of being kind and sociable. Protocol is simply good manners!

Tips On "Social Graces":

- First and foremost be humble, it will pay tremendous dividends.

- Smile, be friendly and look people in the eye (understand that some cultures may view this as disrespectful so know your surroundings and the culture, but on average it is accepted as polite).

- Be polite and approachable and engage in conversation with others. Often times it is best to approach someone that is standing or sitting alone. Chances are they may feel out of place and you may be the spark that starts a wonderful friendship. Who knows, you may even become a great mentor to a younger spouse!

- Never introduce yourself as the spouse of so and so. In other words, if your spouse happens to be in a position of authority or prestige don't take advantage of it. Never introduce yourself as "Lieutenant so and so's spouse" or "First Sergeant so and so's spouse." Simply introduce yourself by your first and last name...*you will be amazed at the respect you will gain from this small effort.*

- If someone happens to introduce you as the spouse of a senior person, you can make a friendly comment like just call me "Jane" or "Joe". This immediately shows that you are not focused on your spouses' position or authority; it also lets people know right away that you are not focused on rank, privilege, or position.

- Do not expect special privileges as a result of your spouse's position or rank. For example, if a military police officer happens to stop you and you are wrong, accept the consequences of your actions! We would encourage you to even go as far as talking with the officer's superior and thanking them for not treating you different than any other person on the installation. This goes along way and the word will travel fast that you are without a doubt a down to earth person who will accept responsibility for your actions...*it sends a significant message to others who may believe that prestige and power are more important than anything else.*

- Refrain from making negative comments about other spouses (or people in general). If you don't have anything positive to say, say nothing at all.

THE MILITARY SPOUSE

- Understand that you are not in the military, but that the military has certain customs and protocols. Use proper courtesy when speaking to individuals who are senior to your spouse by saying Ma'am or Sir. If they wish for you to call them by their first name ***they will insist on it more than once.***

- Understand that the more senior in grade your spouse is, the more your actions or inactions will be observed. The best advice here is treat people like you want to be treated, and do what's right even when no one else is watching. Believe me, the first time you do something that is even perceived as unethical, immoral, unkind or illegal it will travel like wild fire. If you conduct yourself in a professional manner your honor will always be above reproach.

- As your spouse becomes senior in grade, there will be more and more social events to attend. While it is not a requirement for you to attend such functions, it is a definite plus if you do. It shows that you support him/her, that you care not only about the installation and its personnel, but also the community as a whole. Be willing to give of yourself as much as possible. This will vary depending on your family commitments, financial matters (formals, dinners, and evenings out are not usually cheap), employment status, etc. You may not be able to make all the events but try to make some that are of interest to you, something you enjoy, and demonstrate your interest in the community.

- Do not feel compelled to participate in functions, but do not feel intimidated by them either. Junior or less experienced spouses may look to you for guidance in social skills. It is your choice!

- The earlier in your military experience you become involved in your military community, the better educated you will become.

- Don't worry about not having all the right answers. You can find the answers. Sometimes a younger spouse just needs someone to listen to.

PATRICIA GERECHT & MARK GERECHT

- If you are a junior or less experienced spouse, watch other spouses of more senior service members and decide which ones you would like to emulate. Follow their lead. Ask them questions. Learn from their experience!

- As a spouse, you may or may not have a job, but you should find a way to volunteer some of your time to better the community or help service members and their families. Being sincere is key, as *volunteerism without sincerity is worthless.* You may have a lot on your plate...raising a family or a career, but pick out something you enjoy that can better the community even it is only 4 hours a month. *Do something and do it quietly (not for show)!* Your actions will set an example and it will be greatly appreciated by service members and other spouses.

- <u>Listen twice as much as you speak</u>....you can learn a lot about people by being an active listener. *Do not openly share personal information.* Save those conversations for your close friends.

- Do not be afraid to entertain in your home.

- Certain subjects are taboo: Politics, religion, military deployments or operations your spouse may be engaged in (remember **security** is paramount to the safety of our service members) or other controversial subjects. Try never to gossip. *A good rule of thumb is that those who gossip **to you** will gossip **about you**.*

- When attending social functions, do not assume you will be placed in a position of honor, be humble sit in the back or wait to have someone direct you to your seat. There is nothing more embarrassing than assuming you're important only to be asked to give up your seat to a more senior person. <u>Let others honor you...do not honor yourself...less you send the wrong message that you are demanding respect.</u> Demanding respect can create animosity among spouses and military members. *You and your*

THE MILITARY SPOUSE

spouse may hold a position of prestige, but your seating arrangement may vary from event to event depending on who else attends. Always check the seating chart if you have RSVP'd. In addition, if by chance you are not on the seating chart be humble and find a seat in the rear of the event....it will speak volumes of your character. If you did not RSVP do not assume the host should have planned for your arrival anyway.

- If you are unsure of what to do at a function, watch and observe others. Try to find a senior spouse or military member, observe their actions then you have an idea of how to proceed.

- In some social circles there is a distinct difference made between Officer and NCO spouses. *Avoid this at all costs.* You want to be seen as a team builder. Among spouses rank and position should not matter. What matters is that spouses form a team to help the unit and community. If we focus on rank we all lose, and you will build walls of animosity instead of building bridges among spouses of all ranks. *No spouse has rank - we are all in this together.*

- You should be very careful about discussing work issues or items your spouse may have shared with you. This fuels the rumor mill. *Our advice is never talk about your spouses' job/work or his/her conversations.*

- At socials you may be tempted to stay close to someone you know. It's a natural instinct. Instead, try to socialize and more than likely others will introduce you to people. Use this as an opportunity to build a bridge and develop a friendship. Grow your network of friends and contacts. *Pick someone to talk to who looks more uncomfortable than you feel and you will both benefit.*

- Family Readiness Group Leaders (FRG): If you are the senior spouse in the unit do not feel compelled to be the Family Readiness Group Leader. That job is best left to a willing and eager volunteer. You can do the job if you wish but be careful not to impose your will on the group. If someone else volunteers and appears to have the right qualities then they should be placed in the position. This is a decision made by the Commander, not the spouse. If someone else is the FRG Leader, offer to help and provide positive support.

Note: For clarification purposes we fully understand that some individuals will attempt to utilize their spouse's rank or position. The key is to ensure you do not fall into this trap. Be polite and professional with these individuals but do not be intimidated by them.

Key Terms:

- **Change of Command:** An event in which a Commander relinquishes command of a unit and passes the duties and responsibilities to another Commander. Traditionally this is symbolized by the passing of the unit colors between the incoming and outgoing Commanders and their superior officer. An RSVP is usually requested.

- **Change of Responsibility:** Similar to the change of command but is usually reserved for enlisted personnel in the rank of First Sergeant and Command Sergeant's Major or high ranking civilian positions. The Commander of the unit typically honors the departing enlisted service member by thanking them for their service and charges the incoming enlisted leader with the duties and responsibilities of executing the mission, and overseeing the health and welfare of the enlisted service members.

- **Dining In:** Traditional dinner for military members of an organization or unit. Spouses are not invited to attend these events. These events are typically designed to build camaraderie among the members of the unit.

- **Dining Out:** Similar to a dining in, but spouses, family members, and guests are invited. Rich in tradition and a time to have some

THE MILITARY SPOUSE

fun. Check the invitation for the dress requirements. These are usually formal.

- **Hail and Farewell:** An event, usually informal and in the evening, that welcomes newcomers to a unit and says good bye to departing individuals. Spouses are usually invited.

- **Receiving lines:** A formal way for a host or hostess to greet guests and to introduce dignitaries in the line. A word about receiving lines: it is very important to be on time! Many times an entire unit will go through together.

- **Rules for a receiving line:**

    o When a couple stands in the line, the ladies go before men even if both people are in the military (exception: Air Force or White house function).

    o No food, drinks, or cigarettes in the line.

    o Never shake the Adjutant's or Aide's hand - *they will be the 1st person you come to in the line and* will usually keep their hands behind their back to avoid any confusion....You will provide your name to the Aide and it will be passed down the line.

    o Do not carry on long conversations in the line.

    o Keep the lines moving.

    o If someone has problems pronouncing your name, it is proper to state your name and if you did not hear a name, it is proper to ask the person to repeat their name.

Teas and Coffees: Our intent is to provide an overall view and provide different ideas. **Be sure to invite male spouses of military**

personnel, because they may want to attend. Remember that the goal is to make everyone part of the team. Our recommendation (with the command's approval) is to invite all ranks (Enlisted and Officers).

Everyone has something to contribute. *It is also the perfect way to assist younger spouses in learning how to hold, prepare, and conduct an event. In addition it let them know you care and help them relax.* The goal is to form a team and a unified support network for each other.

- Have a written agenda for the event. Perhaps the first coffee or tea would focus on:

    o Would we like this to be a monthly or quarterly event?

    o How would we like to pay for it (does it fall to the hostess alone, or does everyone contribute)?

    o Do you use it as an opportunity to hail new spouses and farewell departing spouses?

- If you are invited, be sure to RSVP either "yes" or "no", unless the invitation specifically states that you need not respond if you do not plan to attend.

- Sometimes formal is good, but if you want people to relax, get to know one another, and be motivated to come back…perhaps informal is better.

- Play a game or two in which you are required to find out something interesting about another spouse. Or have everyone write down something they believe no one else would know about them. Put them all in a jar and have someone pull them out one at a time and read them…then the rest of the spouses try to guess who this person might be. Another suggestion would be to have everyone bring a wedding photo and try to guess who is who.

THE MILITARY SPOUSE

- We have found events like coffees and teas that are more productive if they are fun, informal, and organized.

- It is a good idea to have name tags for a new event, or when numerous people may not know each other. This helps people feel like they can approach others.

- Share information about critical dates on the installation and unit calendar. Plan for welcome homes for service members returning from training. Imagine this…the spouses meet the service members as they return from 30 days of training away from home station…cooking hamburgers/hot dogs, with cold sodas. With such a scenario, family members get the chance to see what recovery from training looks like and children get a feel for what their parents do. Imagine the impact that would have on a group of returning service members, all because you cared and planned something while you were at a coffee/tea. By the way, your group will feel good about their achievement and know it was a team effort focused on supporting the service member.

- **A note on keeping rosters**: Some rosters may contain personal information such as martial status, names of dependents, salaries, home addresses, and phone numbers. *Remember this information cannot be released to third parties without the consent of the individual.* For example, you may receive a call from one spouse asking for the number of another spouse. Our recommendation would be to offer to call the spouse in question and pass the message on along with the phone number of the individual that is requesting the information. This way you do not release the information and the message is passed to the individual concerned. It is up to the spouse receiving the information to decide if he/she wants to return the call. *Remember to treat this information as you would want your private information handled..*

How Should I Eat That? You may think at home certain foods are definitely finger foods…but you may be surprised at how items should be eaten at formals! Here are some suggestions:

The following are considered finger foods:

- Artichokes, asparagus (if they are fresh and small).

- Bacon: if crisp use your fingers, other wise use a knife and fork.

- Chicken: knife and fork, sometimes fried chicken will be eaten with your fingers.

- Corn on cob: What do you mean I have to cut the corn from the cob and then eat it? That's work. At some dinners you may be able to eat it directly from the cob. Watch what others are doing.

These are just a few examples but the bottom line is look to your left and right if you have doubts….look at the head table…and follow suit.

When It's Time To Eat: Usually the head table or senior people will be asked go to the serving line or they will be served first. *<u>A nice touch we have seen in the past is when the senior person present stops and states…".I believe we should allow our enlisted guests to go first followed by our other distinguished guests</u>*." Again it sends a message *of* **<u>servant leadership</u>**. While in the field Army leaders typically have the young service members to eat first…before the senior service members; this ensures the junior service members are well fed….if there is not enough food, the seniors go without. Actions like these truly touch a service members' heart.

How Should I Dress? Good question and perhaps you should ask yourself how you would like to be perceived by the audience at the event. You see, just because it is in fashion at the local dance hall or other places you may choose to go to, it does not mean it is appropriate for a military

THE MILITARY SPOUSE

function. *In addition, understand that you are not only representing your spouse but also the military.* Wearing garments that expose too much, improperly cover or attract unwelcome attention should not be worn. If it is that short or that sexy, save if for another occasion. Regardless of the event (formal or informal) dress in a conservative manner. Be a lady or a gentleman, and show it by how you dress and act.

The following information and tables are an extract from DA PAM 600-60 Chapter 8 and should assist you in determining the proper type of dress for an event:

- Proper dress for a military or social function. The guidance shown in table 8-1 is for Army personnel to use in choosing the proper dress while attending a military or social function. The occasions, accessories, insignia, and accouterments, see AR 670-1. Table 8-2 provides guidance on the dress codes normally used today.

- Tie worn with Army blue and Army white uniforms. The four in hand tie is worn with the Army blue and Army white uniforms at functions that begin in the afternoon and before the hour of retreat. The host may prescribe either the four in hand or bow tie for evening affairs according to the degree of formality.

- Wear of the Army white uniform: The Army white uniform may be worn as prescribed by local commanders in areas that require this uniform (AR 670-1), or in other areas as the individual wishes.

- Equivalent uniforms of Army and other services: Table 8-3 and table 8-4 contain the uniform equivalency and occasions for wear by males and females in the Army, Marine Corps, Navy/Coast Guard, and Air Force. It also contains the appropriate attire for female and male civilian spouse/escorts.

Table 8-1 Army Uniform/Civilian Attire

Occasion/Function	Civilian Attire	Army Uniform	Ladies Attire
Ceremonies, parades, reviews, official visits of foreign dignitaries	Coat and Tie	Army Blue with Four in Hand Tie, Army Green	Afternoon Dress/suit
Receptions, daytime or early evening semi-formal occasions requiring more than duty uniform	Dark business suit	Army Blue with Bow tie or Four in hand tie	Cocktail Dress
Official Formal Functions (black tie)	Dinner Jacket/Tuxedo	Army Blue White, or Black Mess/Army Blue with bowtie	Long or Short Evening Dress
Official Formal Evening Functions (White Tie)	Tails	Army Blue, or Black Evening Mess	Evening Formal

Note 1: The Army white/Army white mess/Army white evening mess uniforms may be substituted for the Army blue equivalent uniforms from April to October, except in clothing zones 1 and 2 where they may be worn year round.

Table 8-2 Dress Code

Category	Dress
Formal (White Tie)	Blue/white evening mess
Semiformal (Black Tie)	Blue/white mess; Army blue with bow tie Army blue w/four in hand (Note 1)
Uniform Informal	Army Green (Note 2)
Duty Uniform	Civilian coat and tie
Civilian Informal Casual	Civilian open collar or sweater w/coat
Very Casual	Shirt and Slacks

Notes: 1 enlisted personnel may wear the army green uniform with black bow tie, and white shirt 2, or uniform dictated by local policy.

Table 8-3 Uniform Comparison Chart for Men

Occasions/ Functions	Army	Marine Corps	Navy /Coast Guard	Air Force	Civilian Attire
Ceremonies parades reviews, official visits of civilian dignitaries, change of command	Army Green Uniform, General Duty wear	Service uniform General wear	Service dress uniform general wear	Service dress uniform general wear	Business suit
Receptions; daytime/early evening formal or semi formal (no bow tie required)	Army Blue/ White Uniform Wear at general official/social occasions	Blue Dress A or B and White Dress A or B Wear at general official/ social occasions	Full Dress uniforms Wear at general official social occasions	Blues or Service Dress will usually be specified. Semi formal may also be specified	Dark Business suit
Social function of general or official nature black tie	Army blue/White Mess Equivalent to black tie	Evening dress B or Mess Dress uniform Equivalent to black tie	Dinner Dress uniform equivalent to black tie	Mess Dress Uniform Black tie occasions	Dinner Jacket/ tuxedo
Official formal evening state event white tie	Army Blue Evening Mess Equivalent to white tie	Evening Dress a uniform equivalent to white tie	Formal Dress Uniform equivalent to white tie	Mess Dress uniform equivalent to white tie	Tuxedo/ tails

Table 8-4 Uniform Comparison Chart for Women

Occasion/ Function	Army	Marine Corps	Navy/ Coast Guard	Air Force	Civilian Attire
Ceremonies parades reviews visits of civilian dignitaries change of command	Army Green Uniform General Duty wear	Service Uniform General Wear	Service Dress Uniform General Wear	Service Dress Uniform General Wear	Afternoon dress/suit
Receptions daytime early evening formal or semi-formal (no bow tie required)	Army Blue White Uniform Wear at general official /social occasions	Blue Dress A or B and White Dress A or B wear at general official/ social occasions	Full dress uniforms wear at official/ ceremonial occasions	Blues or Service Dress will usually be specified. Semi formal may also be specified	Afternoon dress/suit; cocktail dress
Social Function of General or Official Nature Black Tie	Army Blue/ White Mess equivalent to Black tie	Evening Dress B or Mess Dress uniform Equivalent to Black tie	Dinner Dress Uniform Equivalent to Black Tie	Mess Dress Uniform For Black tie occasions	Long or Short Evening Dress
Official formal evening; state event white tie	Army Blue Evening Mess Equivalent to white tie	Evening Dress A uniform Equivalent to white tie	Formal Dress Uniform Equivalent to white tie	Mess Dress Uniform (white tie/wing tip collar) Equivalent to white tie	Long Evening Dress

How to Dress:

- The way you dress depends on what the invitation reads. If in doubt, call the hostess.

- Formal - Long or short formal gown for a ball or dance. Formal is defined by length. A long formal is to the floor, and a short formal is calf or ankle length. It matters not how "glitzy" a gown is, as long as it is proper length. A long dress, or blouse/skirt set is appropriate for a dinner.

- Informal - A dressy suit or dress.

- Coat and Tie - Simple dress, blouse/skirt set, pantsuit- a little dressier than work clothing.

- Casual - Simple dress, blouse/skirt set, pantsuit.

- Very casual - Slacks, jeans, blouse, sweater...you may even be told shorts, but NO cut-offs!

- If still in doubt, dress up rather than down.

Invitations:

- *Responding to invitations*

    o It is important to remain courteous to a hostess by responding to an invitation both in the manner specified, and in a timely manner, usually within 48 hours.

    o RSVP - French abbreviation for "respondez sail vous plait" or in plain English – "please respond." If this is on your invitation, reply within 48 hours and let your hostess know if you plan to attend or not and definitely no later than 48 hours before the event. Respond Yes or No.

THE MILITARY SPOUSE

- o Regrets Only - Reply in a reasonable amount of time only if you do not plan to attend. If you do not respond at all the hostess will count on your attending.

- o If you first respond to an invitation and then later find your situation changes, please inform your hostess. For example, if you can not go, and then later find you can, do not just show up. Inform your hostess, for she or he may have adjusted the evening to your absence, and showing up might cause problems. Many times you will find that you are still welcomed. In addition, if you RSVP'd "yes" then cannot attend please call and inform the host or hostess.

Thank-You Notes:

- Try to always send your hostess a thank you note as soon as possible after a function. The following are guidelines to help you in writing your thank you notes:

    - o Address note to both the host and hostess.

    - o Only the person writing the note signs it.

    - o Send the note promptly!

    - o Something to consider including in your note:
        - Something about the meal, or what was served.
        - Address the hospitality, and then the mention your host.
        - Include a final sentence expressing your thanks, and a formal compliment.

    - o Thank you cards: Are best hand written, as it shows sincerity and that you took the time to add a personal touch.

- o Try to have more than three sentences in your written note.

An Example to Go By:

> March 5, 2004
>
> Dear Mr. and Mrs. Bravo,
>
> Joe and I would like to thank you and Major Bravo for having us over for dinner Saturday evening. We greatly enjoyed the dinner and your company. It was a great to meet the other spouses in the unit. We greatly appreciate you thinking of us.
>
> Respectfully,
>
> Jane Doe

Notice That:

- She included the date
- Should be written by hand
- She included her husband in the note (Joe)
- She also mentioned the host (Major Bravo)
- She talked about what she liked

TIP: Keep a blank set of thank-you-notes in your car with stamps affixed. When you leave an event you can quickly fill out the card and drop it in the mail as on your way home. Don't forget to write the address down before you leave the event location.

THE MILITARY SPOUSE

CHAPTER 7
DEALING WITH DEPLOYMENTS

It is always difficult to say good bye! It is even more difficult for children, no matter what the situation, whether a normal training rotation or a real world deployment. Here are some ideas and suggestions that may help spouses and children during these difficult situations.

Support Agencies, Programs And Mechanisms: Families have access to several support agencies. Each service offers them and they include: Army Community Service, Navy and Marine Corps Family Service Centers, and Air Force Family Support Centers also known as Family Services. These agencies provide personal and family readiness support to service members, Commanders, and families during deployments and times of need. They offer additional services to keep families informed, connected and provides assistance in coping with stressful circumstances.

TIP: We strongly recommend that you call ACS first and then go visit them. This provides them an opportunity to understand your needs or desires; therefore, they can be better prepared to assist you.

- **The Red Cross:** Usually provides a link to and from the service member to notify and verify that an emergency situation has occurred and a message is sent to the service member's chain of command requesting that the service member be granted emergency leave or be advised of a situation.

- **United States Service Organization (USO):** The USO's mission is to provide morale, welfare and recreation-type services to uniformed military personnel. There are about 120 USO Centers around the world. Programs and services include: "newcomer" briefings for troops and family members, family crisis counseling, support groups for families separated by deployments, housing assistance, libraries and reading rooms, cultural awareness seminars, airport service centers, recreational activities, nursery facilities, high-quality inexpensive tours, new spouse orientations, telephone capabilities, as well as internet and e-mail capabilities. USO centers on or off base provide a relaxing and wholesome alternative to daily stress.

- **Installation or base chapel:** Provide support for most religious beliefs and can be helpful in finding a local place of worship. Conducts youth related activities, provides religious study sessions and counseling, and is usually available for military weddings.

- **Family Assistance Centers (FAC):** During deployments Commanders *may* establish consolidated family assistance centers to provide centralized support to families. Centers may connect you with ACS, chaplains, lawyers, Army Emergency Relief, TRICARE, military personnel, and finance. The centers are usually only established when a large force is deployed and not for individual service members.

- **Military One Source:** A 24 hours 7 day a week toll free information and referral telephone service. It is available to active duty, Guard, and Reserve service members, deployed civilians and their families worldwide. Provides information from minor concerns to deployment and return issues. Can provide contact with professional civilian counselors if there is a need for face to face counseling. Call: 1-800-464-8107.

- **Army Family and Soldier Readiness System:** Consists of family readiness groups, rear detachment commanders, and family assistance centers. Also provides assistance to local National Guard and reserve units that are deployed in the local area.

- **MyArmyLifeToo.com:** Provides family members with up to date and accurate articles and information on numerous topics including Army customs, relocation tips, home and personal safety guidance,

THE MILITARY SPOUSE

and financial management. Serves as a one stop knowledge center for family members. It has forums and chat rooms, managed by staff or subject matter experts.

- **Operation Ready:** Education resources about deployment preparing the active duty, National Guard, Reserve service members and families for deployments, redeployments, and reunions.

- **OP Ready for Kids:** Helps children express issues surrounding a parent's deployment. It includes age appropriate material for children from preschool to high school. Items include story and activity books, for younger children, comic books and a teen magazine for older children.

- **New Parent Support Program Plus:** Home visitation for new parents to help provide a positive parenting environment. Primary audience is first time parents and individuals and couples at high risk.

- **Transitional Compensation for Abused Dependents:** Part of the National Defense Authorization Act of FY94, helps individuals come forward to report abuse. Provides temporary payments for qualifying individuals. Rates are specified for dependency and indemnity compensation to families in which the service member has been discharged administratively or court martialed or has forfeited all pay and allowances as a result of disciplinary actions for dependent abuse. Commissary, dental, and medical service, and exchange privileges remain in effect during the benefit period.

- **Employment Readiness:** Provides every spouse the opportunity to develop or maintain a career or employment. Builds partnerships with Department of Defense, Federal agencies, private corporations and non profit organizations concerning training, career continuity and retirement benefits for military spouses.

- **Exceptional Family Member Program (EFMP):** Enrollment is mandatory for individuals who have special needs or disabilities. This program works with other military and civilian agencies to provide all types of support including: housing, medical, educational, and community support to families with special needs. A service member will not normally be assigned to an installation or post in which their EMFP family member cannot receive adequate care. However, the service member may request an exception to this policy thru their respective assignment management agency.

- **Financial Readiness Program:** Educational counseling program for personal financial management for service members and their families. Teaches how to live within your means, secure a financial future and help foster self reliance.

- **Relocation Readiness Program:** Helps service members and families deal with the problems, issues, and stress of moving. Can provide information on almost any subject at the gaining duty station or installation.

- **Army Family Team Building:** Over 40 classes are available on stress management, customs, courtesies, and acronyms. The objective of the program is to teach personal and family readiness through sequential training. This training is for everyone, the newly married spouse and seasoned spouses. Other services may offer a similar program.

- **Army Family Action Plan:** Seeks input from all components with regard to well being issues. These issues are compiled at the local level and elevated to higher levels of leadership. It helps leaders understand what programs are needed and what areas are being successfully addressed. You have a voice in this program…use it to better your community.

- **Family Advocacy Program:** Promotes community awareness by teaching individuals to understand, identify, and report child abuse and/or spousal abuse. The Army Community Service Center *(or similar sister service organization)* has the primary responsibility for managing this program.

- **Virtual Family Readiness Group:** Helps provide information to family members who are dispersed. It also includes access for families and significant others or single service members. It provides the functionality of a traditional family readiness group online.

- **Child and Youth Services: Many installations, bases and/or posts have the following services available:**
    - Full Day Care
    - Part Day Care
    - Shift Care
    - Hourly Care
    - Youth Programs
    - Extended Hours Care
    - Around the Clock Care
    - Respite Care
    - Back Up Child Care Homes
    - On Site Group Care
    - Child Development Centers
    - Family Child Care Homes
    - School Age Centers
    - Youth Centers and Teen Centers
    - Child and Youth Service Liaison, Education and Outreach Services
    - Youth Education Support Services
    - Outreach Services
    - Student to Student
    - Operation Proud Partners

How To Cope:

- Develop a sound foundation of friends you can TRUST!

- Don't become involved in GOSSIP!

- Become involved in the community.

- Support your unit spouse organization.

- Consider having your spouse make a **video tape** of him/her:

    o Reading your **child's favorite story** – *note be sure to keep the book with the tape.*

    o Saying **bedtime prayers** with the children.

    o Making special recordings for **birthdays, graduations, and other significant events** that you can play for the child when the day comes if your spouse won't be there.

- If the deployment location permits, *arrange a time to call home* every week. If access to a computer is available utilize a web cam on the computer so you can have a live discussion with the family, or instant messages at a prescribed time. ACS, FAC's, or other similar agencies in our sister services may have a webcam for family members to use as well.

- If your spouse is deployed close to a unit that has **video tele-conferencing (VTC)** capability, see if you can partner with a unit on your installation to set up a VTC for the spouses to speak with their loved ones that are deployed. *We understand that Air Force Family Services and Army Community Service may assist in supporting these efforts.*

THE MILITARY SPOUSE

- Buy your spouse some **special mailing envelopes**: Perhaps a bright color. If it is a training deployment, put stamps on them. Then when you open the mail box you will know right away you have a letter from your spouse…just by the color of the envelope.

- Understand that communications will not always be the best, and that sometimes locations are very isolated. Do not let a dropped call, or bad connection bother you.

- Try not to watch the news or focus on negative reports coming out of the area of action. Try to focus on other aspects of your life and family. It is natural to worry but worrying won't help…it will more than likely make you feel worse. A good suggestion we received was to only watch the first 10 minutes of the news in the morning, afternoon, and evening. This is normally where the news is and after this timeframe the coverage tends to be more speculative or opinion based…which can increase anxiety.

- Put a yellow ribbon outside your home: Think about the level of safety in your neighborhood. You may not wish to display a yellow ribbon openly. It could signal to a criminal that you may be home alone and therefore possibly and easier target. If you choose to hang a yellow ribbon, be sure you evaluate the impact on your personal safety as well as any children that may be under your care.

- Hang a *Blue Star Banner* in your window at home showing that you support your deployed spouse. If you are living alone, with small children, or off the base, it may be wise to display the banner in an area that is not visible from the outside of your home. You may be asking yourself, "Why would I not display the banner openly"? The banner is an indication you may be home alone. Thus, for safety reasons we ask that you consider this suggestion.

- Talk to your children about why your spouse had to leave, provide encouragement, attention and love. Remember children you're your attention.

93

- *Teddy bears help*: During recent deployments several volunteer organizations got together and developed a Christmas Bear program. This program focused on providing families a day of fun, entertainment, and an opportunity to spend some time with other individuals that had loved ones deployed. The main idea was to give each child a teddy bear in a special presentation and encourage them to talk with their bear! The children were told to share their feelings and thoughts with their bear. We received absolutely wonderful comments from numerous parents about this program. Many of them stated that their children became more positive about daily events in general because of the bear and their ability to share their concerns and joys with the bear. *It's just a thought…and it provides another option to try and help children to cope while their loved ones are deployed.*

- Have the service member buy something for your children before they leave, perhaps 12 items. Once a month you can say, "let's have a treasure hunt…Dad or Mom…got us something special and we have to find the clues to get the prize." It could be a DVD, tickets to a movie, having pizza at home…the idea is to allow the children to focus on the fact that just because a parent is away they still CARE and are a part of their life.

- Take time for yourself and try and relax with a friend who also has a deployed spouse.

- Get involved in a local organization that volunteers; helping service members or other service organizations.

Dealing With Deployments: Is handled differently by different families and their unique situation. The important thing to remember is that deployments are only temporary. Plan for separations. Keep your legal documents up to date. Talk with your children. Make plans as best

THE MILITARY SPOUSE

you can. Most importantly, know that there are numerous support agencies available to you on and off base to assist you in helping your children cope and helping you cope. Sometimes taking time to help others is a good way of coping and taking your mind off your personal situation.

Unfortunately there is no one plan that fits all situations. Deployments and redeployments take a toll on the family and you must be ready for them. *One personal example: when we were very young my husband would go away for very long periods of time. One day he came home and I had done several jobs around the house that needed to be done, all things he normally did. That evening he looked at me and said, "I guess you don't need me around much anymore" and when I asked him what he meant, his reply was, "Everything I used to do before I left you do for yourself now!" While he was proud of me for adapting, it was difficult for him because he felt he was no longer needed..*

If you do one thing at all, do this: **plan, talk, and prepare for separations.** Include communication about the following questions:

- What about our finances?
- What happens if there is a medical emergency?
- Who do you contact with a problem?
- Do you have the right contact numbers?
- What agencies are available to help with problems?
- What agency should be my starting point?

Put a book together with all the information you may need, tab it, and make it user friendly. When the deployment comes, there will be less stress, more time to enjoy the family, and most of all…peace of mind.

Support Programs Like Operation Ready: New programs are being developed all the time. Stay in touch with your family readiness group and your local support systems. **Two programs you should check into now are Operation Ready and the Virtual FRG**. *There is a host of information available on the web* concerning these programs and they include information that is important for the Guard and Reserve as well.

Guard and Reserve Components: Face additional issues than those of active duty service members. It has been our experience that internet searches have provided a vast wealth of knowledge that is not well advertised. Do your homework and check into issues.

In addition, we strongly encourage you to contact the nearest military installation. They will typically have some type of support groups on the post, base, or installation. You will find that most want to help, in addition, they are obligated to provide some type of support. Most of all, the individual you will contact in the support agencies truly understand what you are going thru and they sincerely want to help!

Reserve units have family readiness group (FRG) leaders that volunteer their time to support the family members of deployed service members. FRG leaders may:

- Help publish newsletters for the benefit of sharing information about the service members and the unit.

- Maintain contact with family members thru email or phone conversations.

- Maintain contact with the chain of command (rear detachment and at times with the deployed command element, but this is usually discouraged, it is best to handle as many issues as possible by utilizing the rear detachment command team).

- Minimize rumor control by helping to keep clear lines of communication open with family members and the unit command element, discouraging gossiping.

- Help organize family days, fund raising events, morale building events (for example: video teleconferencing sessions with family members and their deployed service member), organize welcome home ceremonies, etc.

- Another individual that may assist Reserve family members during deployments is the Unit Administrator.

In the end it all comes together! If spouses trust each other, are there for one another and understand each other. They will be better equipped to deal with very difficult situations such as loneliness, separation, medical issues, etc. Also understand that at times the service member will seem removed because their job will normally keep their energies focused on their job. On the home front you will normally juggle day to day activities like taking care of the home, children, and worrying about your deployed spouse. Both of you can make it thru deployments but you must do it as a team. The key is to understand, share openly, talk, and be there for each other.

PATRICIA GERECHT & MARK GERECHT

CHAPTER 8
HONEY IT IS TIME TO MOVE

Military life requires tremendous flexibility when it comes to Permanent Change of Station (PCS) or moving. Currently, the military is looking at ways to stabilize families longer in one place rather than moving families every 2-4 years. This may mean that families will stay in one location longer, but that service members may deploy more often and return to the same location, thus providing the family with more stability, and allowing the spouse stability and more potential for a career.

Moving to a new location can be a very enjoyable experience. The opportunity to meet new people, see different countries, and experience different cultures can be an experience of a life time. It is very exciting but you must plan the move, and at times that becomes stressful. In this chapter we will explore ways to make a move as easy as possible.

You can normally expect movement notification between 90 days and 12 months before your travel date. Before we get any further let's get some terms out of the way:

Hold Baggage Or Unaccompanied Baggage: These items consist of items you will need as you move into to your new set of quarters or apartment at your new duty station. These items consist of things like sheets, blankets, pots, pans, a few dishes, perhaps a small T.V. some clothing, a few small toys for the children, towels, wash cloths, etc. These are essential items only. A service member normally receives approval for 500 lbs. of shipping weight allowance, and the spouse and children each receive an additional weight allowance. This shipment is moved quickly and will usually be at the new station upon your arrival or shortly after your arrival. You can pack professional items in this shipment which will not be counted against your total weight allowance. *When moving overseas, you should plan to send this shipment at least six weeks in advance of your travel date. This should ensure you receive it in a timely manner at your new overseas duty location.*

Household Goods: These are items that make up the vast majority of your furniture and clothing. These items can take 45-90 days to arrive depending on the date you ship, the destination, and the amount of leave you take between assignments.

Storage: If you are going overseas you will be offered the ability to put some of your items in storage. These items will be stored for you in the United States until your return. Washers and dryer or refrigerators are good examples of items left for storage.

Good things to Know: Your items must be clean or the movers can refuse to pack them, and they must be free of pests. If your items are dirty and/or are infested with bugs or other such insects you could be charged for an attempted pickup.

Transformers*: No not the cartoon☺!* Some foreign countries operate electric appliances on 220 volts, while in the States most of our appliances operate at 110-120 volts. Most new military housing units overseas come with 110-120 volts. If you live on the *economy*, meaning off post in a town, you will need to buy transformers. They come in different watts for example: 75, 100, 250, 500, 1000, 3000 watts. You may be able to purchase them at your current thrift shop (usually they are cheaper because service members have no use for them in the States), otherwise you can find them at your overseas thrift shop, Post/Base Exchange, or buy them from someone who is leaving the overseas location.

Please keep in mind that each type of shipment hold baggage, household goods, and storage are separate shipments and will normally be picked up on separate days and usually by separate companies. An appointment is required for each shipment. These are all coordinated through your local transportation office. Download a copy *of*

THE MILITARY SPOUSE

DA Pam 55-2 "It's your Move" from the internet. This pamphlet includes things like weight allowances, mover, and service member responsibilities.

Believe it or not you will usually have plenty of time to plan your move. *The Army usually does a good job of giving most service members at least 90 days notice. However, some of our fellow service members in sister services have explained that they have frequently received 60 days or less to move. Therefore it is always a good idea to keep a check list ready in the event you must move on short notice.*

Once you actually receive orders you will need to sit down with your spouse and determine what day you will actually leave the current duty assignment, from that point you can begin to make your arrangements. **It is imperative to contact the transportation office immediately to set up an appointment**, especially if your service has a normal time frame of high volume moves. For example, Army personnel typically have high movement rates in the summer months since the children are out of school. This is not to say that all movements take place in the summer but a large percent usually do. Such a busy moving season fills up the transportation office calendar quickly!

Do It Yourself Move (DITY Move): It is possible to move your household goods by yourself. Under this type of move you pay for all expenses up front, including truck rental, fuel, and all costs to load the truck. You must have the truck weighed empty and weighed when it is fully loaded. This must be done on a certified scale. Your transportation office can help you with this. All DITY moves are usually reviewed very carefully by the military. *In fact many military careers have been ended by personnel making inappropriate claims.* In addition, the money received from a DITY move is reported to the IRS and you will receive documentation from the military as to the amount of money they reported to the IRS and *you must claim this money on your tax return.*

The following checklist is provided to assist you in preparing for the move:

Moving Planner Checklist:

- **Make copies of your travel orders**! (Get as many as you can, and you don't have to pay for them. Have the military run them off for you or use a copy machine in one of the administrative offices. After all, it is military documentation that is required for your move.)

- If you are being **assigned overseas** ensure you make arrangements immediately with your military personnel office to **obtain passports**. In addition, we would recommend that you also obtain a regular U.S. passport in addition to your military passport. Military members are not normally required to have a passport. They are not normally issued a military passport; therefore it is a good idea for them to obtain a regular U.S. passport in the event you plan to travel outside your country of assignment. In addition, the only identification a military member will have to identify themselves is a military ID card. Given the terrorist threats these days it is best to have a U.S. passport.

- When you travel on a plane or outside the U.S. it is a good idea to keep your military ID cards in a place other than your wallet or purse. Do not openly display them. The idea is that you do not want to be readily associated as a military member. This is simply to help you keep a low profile. You would rather someone think you are a tourist rather than a service member or military dependant.

- When traveling on a civilian carrier outside the United States, don't travel in military uniform or wearing clothing that identifies you as a military member. Try to blend in and be inconspicuous. A rule of thumb is that you must not travel in uniform unless your orders state otherwise. However, contact your sponsor at your new location or your current chain of command and find out what the current travel policy states.

- Determine the date you wish to leave housing or terminate your lease.

THE MILITARY SPOUSE

Notify your landlord, rental agent, or housing office of your pending move and projected last date of occupancy. *Check to see if you have a military clause in your lease or rental agreement (which means if your spouse deploys, you receive orders to move to another location, or any other situation in which the military directs a move, then there should be no penalties or extra fees if you need to break the contract.)* **Ensure you check your contract at every duty station for the military clause before you sign it. You can ask for it after the fact, but it will be up to your landlord to grant it.** A military clause is not uncommon and most landlords around military installations are familiar with them. In addition, understand that if your spouse deploys and you wish to return home, this most likely will not be part of your military clause. One last thought on military clauses: get them in writing and make sure they are clearly understood!

Make an appointment with the *Transportation Office* to:

- Estimate weight for your household goods - a good rule of thumb is to assume each room contains approximately 1000 lbs. Using this method you will have a good number to work with. Don't forget to think about garages, workshops, or other areas that may contain many hidden items or extremely heavy ones.

- **Find out what your authorized weight allowance is.** You will have to pay extra for anything above your weight allowance that you ship or store. Get rid of anything you do not want anymore. Consider trying to sell the items at the base/post Thrift Shop or give them to Goodwill, the Salvation Army or other charitable organizations.

- **Determine what items will go in which shipment**. We used a system that utilized stickers: green dots for household goods, and yellow dots for hold baggage items, and red dots for storage. We could then tell the movers to take things only marked with that color.

Lesson Learned: *If you have small children keep the stickers away from them or you will end up with stickers everywhere, and you will also have some very confused movers!*

- **Homeowners or renters insurance:** Check to see if your insurance covers any damages incurred during shipment. If not, you should consider buying insurance that will cover your property during your move or the storage period.

- Put anything you plan to take with you (in your luggage or mail separately) on your trip in an empty room or closet and lock it so the movers cannot pack it by accident.

- Separate all **your important paperwork**. Place passports, ID cards, insurance paperwork, orders, etc. in a separate location. You could possibly store them in your car on moving day to prevent them from being packed up...having these items packed has been known to happen.

- Ensure your trash cans are empty. Movers have been known to pack trash...not a pleasant smell as you open that box. *Movers may even pack a live plant!*

- **Watch the movers** as they **pack** things. Ensure that all high dollar items are properly documented on the inventory sheet.

- **Items that are easily stolen:** Ensure that any items that are easily stolen are properly listed on inventory sheets. These include items such as: computer games, CDs, video games, DVD, and VHS tapes.

- Ensure that packers do not inadvertently mark your belongings as scratched, chipped, dented, or broken. This saves them money if they damage the property during the move.

- Make arrangement with your housing office or landlord for a pre-inspection and a final inspection date.

THE MILITARY SPOUSE

- Are you **shipping a vehicle**? Ship it early, so that it can be waiting on you when you arrive. Internet tracking of your vehicle is available. This information will be made available to you when you process your vehicle for shipment. Decide if you need your vehicle more here or on the other end. Our experience has been to ship a vehicle early, because we could usually find a way around at our current location. You should also find out if you will need to take a written driver's examination at your overseas location. Normally it is a requirement. Your sponsor can provide you with a book and it normally has sample tests in it. In fact, currently, you can usually find the sample tests online by going to the main webpage for the major command you will be assigned to overseas and searching under driver's test, driver's training, or driver's license. In addition, make sure that your stateside driver's license is valid (normally a requirement to get a license overseas), and check the expiration date. If it will expire while you are away, see if you can renew it early. Each state has different rules. For example; in some states you do not need to renew your driver's license as long as you remain in the service, while others will allow you to renew your license thru the mail, while others will require the renewal to take place in person. If you are returning to the States from an overseas tour, we recommend you ship your vehicle early so that it can be picked up as soon as possible. You may be entitled to obtain storage of a vehicle at government expense while deployed or overseas, so check with your transportation office.

- **If your vehicle is not paid for or if it is leased** you will have to obtain permission to have it released to go overseas. You will need a letter from the lien holder.

- Do you have a CB radio or radar detector? You may need to check to see if they are legal in the state or country you are moving to.

- Can you ship personal firearms, and/or are you authorized to ship equipment for reloading ammunition? Are cross bows authorized for shipment?

- Make sure your valuables are appraised in advance and that you take out special insurance for these items. Be sure they are specifically listed on your inventory as valuables, antiques, etc.

- Another excellent idea is to clearly mark 1 or 2 boxes for items like tools, furniture hardware, toilet paper, personal grooming items, medicines, bedding, toys, paper plates, cups, etc. This allows you to quickly identity the boxes during your move in and will help you get unpacked and organized quicker.

- Your vehicle must be cleaned <u>very well</u> on the inside and outside to include vents, door jams, and wheel wells. Customs will reject cars not properly cleaned. If you clean your car well and drive thru a mud puddle or bad weather before you drop your car off for shipping don't be surprised if your vehicle is rejected. Be sure your gas tank has less than ¼ of a tank of gas. The shipping agency will not take the car if it has more than ¼ of a tank...

  Lesson Learned: If the gas tank is too full, you will be driving forever to burn the fuel or pay a lot of money to have someone drain your fuel tank! ☺

- Contact your **car insurance** company and make arrangements to have insurance coverage while your vehicle is in transit to its new location and upon your arrival.

- **Are you shipping a pet?** The government will currently pay up to $275 to help defray the cost of quarantining pets. Quarantine can range from a few days to 6 months. Check before you ship!

- Is there a **pet restriction** in the area you are moving to? Currently known restriction areas include: Iceland, Great Britain, Guam, and Hawaii.

- If you own a **boat, trailer or RV** discuss these matters with your

THE MILITARY SPOUSE

transportation counselor. Certain restrictions apply.

- Backwards plan your move from the date you wish to leave your home and schedule your pick up dates for household goods, unaccompanied baggage, storage items, and inspection dates. Remember, you will be competing with other families and service members for moving dates. So plan ahead and get your dates locked in.

Tips For Moving:

- Contact your sponsor at your new duty station as soon as possible with all your questions about the new location and command.

- Make lodging arrangements locally and on the other end as soon as you have orders in hand.

- Visit your local ACS office and get a relocation packet and information from the SITES database about your new location.

- Visit the website for your new installation.

- Check school schedules and enrollment requirements at your new duty station or local school system.

- Check expiration dates on your military ID and those of your children; update if necessary.

- Understand that anything you personally pack, the moving company will try to write the letters "PBO" on the box, meaning packed by owner. This means they are not responsible for damage with those items. Therefore, if you are packing valuables, leave the box open and explain they are free to repack it but not to place the letters PBO on the box or on the inventory form. You give them the option to accept it or repack it. Normally they will accept your packing method.

- Contact department of motor vehicles upon arriving at your new duty station reference driver's license and vehicle registration.

- Conduct all auto maintenance and repairs prior to departure.

- Contact your insurance company concerning vehicles, renters insurance, home insurance.

- Consider taking out additional insurance for your personal property during the move.

- *Take close up pictures and video tape all valuable property. Hand carry photos and videos do not let the movers pack them.*

- **Record serial numbers** of all valuable property, and carry that information with you.

- Separate all professional books, papers and uniforms, equipment. *They will not be counted against your weight allowance. The weight allowance for professional items can be obtained from your transportation office; an approximation is 500 lbs.*

- **Get appraisals** for expensive and valuable items, such as artwork, collectibles and heirlooms. The government will not pay for the appraisals but you will need them if you want to file for full value or loss/damage of the item.

- **Do not ship small extremely valuable items** such as stocks, bonds, jewelry, coins, coin collections, or items of great sentimental value, such as picture albums. Pack them yourself and hand carry them or mail them to your destination address.

- If you are being assigned to an overseas location, check with your transportation office to see if there are any shipment **weight restrictions** for that area.

THE MILITARY SPOUSE

- If you are going to a weight restricted area the government will store the remainder of your property or ship it to a designated location for the duration of your overseas tour, up to your full weight allowance at government expense.

- **Ensure the packers place a copy of your orders (or a piece of paper with your name and contact information) in each box.** This will help in the event that a box is misplaced or separated from the shipment and it also provides the moving company with an easy method to return your property. *You may request extra copies of your orders be printed or you can make the copies yourself at your office. You should not have to pay to make copies. If you have a concern about identity theft since your orders usually contain social security numbers, just black them out, or simply place a piece of paper inside each box that has your new unit address your name and contact information..*

- Fill out change of address cards for the IRS, Post Office, magazines, bills, etc.

- Keep all medical prescriptions in their original bottles. Obtain prescription slips in case you need refills on the road. Pack medicine in leak proof, spill proof containers.

- If possible, hand carry all medical, dental and finance records (currently the military is getting away from giving medical records to individuals and going to a fully electronic system). Either way, it does not hurt to ask.

    Note:
    - Spouses cannot pick up medical records of each other without written permission and a copy of the ID card for the individual concerned. Depending on your medical facility the adult may be required to pick up the records in person.

- o Some military medical facilities are transitioning to electronic records and you will not receive a copy.

- Ensure your entire family is listed in the Defense Eligibility Enrollment Reports Systems (DEERS).

- Once you are notified of a pending move begin using up any frozen and perishable foods you have on hand. Whatever you are unable to use, share it with neighbors or individuals in need.

- Dispose of flammables such as fireworks, cleaning fluids, matches, acids, chemistry sets, aerosol cans, ammunition, oil, paint and paint thinners, or any other hazardous material that cannot be shipped.

- Drain fuel from mowers/other machinery and clean off all the dirt.

- Discard partly used cans and containers of liquids that may leak.

- Carefully tape and place in waterproof bags any jars of liquid you plan to carry with you.

- Refillable tanks must be purged and sealed by a local propane gas dealer. Discard non refillable tanks. Some carriers and the military do not permit shipment of any propane tanks.

- Notify utility services of your pending move and the date to terminate service including: electric, water, newspaper, magazine, telephone, cable, etc.

- Have appliances cleaned and serviced for the move.

- Clean rugs and clothing prior to the move.

- Plan for any special needs for your travel time, such as for infants (formula, diapers, etc).

- Close bank accounts if required.

- Clear any safe deposit boxes.

- Make copies of all important documents and secure them in two separate locations.

- Defrost freezer and refrigerator. Place deodorizer inside the appliances to control odors.

- Ensure you label or tag any item that is to be left in the dwelling, so that the movers do not pack it (example: oven, refrigerator, etc). Better yet, if possible, put it in a closet or separate room and lock the door.

- Ensure that you properly drain all the water out of your washer by tipping it on its side. Water left in the machine can cause serious problems if the washer is to be left in storage for a significant period of time.

- Provide an extended family member, or someone not traveling with you with a copy of the route you plan to travel (itinerary).

- Discuss the moving process with your family. Focus on the positives of the new location. If your child(ren) play sports make early contact with coaches at the next duty station. This is ***extremely*** important!

- Return library books and any other borrowed items.

- Pets:
    - Make arrangements for transporting pets.

- Some airlines will only ship pets during certain months and/or temperature ranges. Check with airlines.

- Carry health and rabies certificates with you. Some countries require health certificates be issued within 10 days of the travel date.

- Ask about vaccinations needed to travel to foreign countries.

- Attach an ID tag to your pet's collar with current contact information listed on it.

- Check on type and size of kennel needed for overseas shipment.

- You can check for pet friendly hotels on the web at www.petswelcome.com.

- **Moving out day:**

  - Double check all closets, drawers, shelves, attic, and garage to be sure they are empty. Designate one area as a storage area for the items you will take with you. _Lock this area._

  - If you have small children arrange for a baby sitter.

  - Carry travelers checks or use credit/debit cards, but be sure to have some cash on hand.

    Lesson Learned: *When traveling overseas have plenty of $1 bills available.* We usually did this when we traveled on vacation to other countries. It came in handy as a tip and believe it or not, some vendors did not want to give back change. They would prefer you simply pick out something else instead of providing change. In some countries they would rather be paid in U.S. dollars than in the local currency.

THE MILITARY SPOUSE

- o Watch the loading and unloading of all your property.

- o Ensure all boxes are labeled with the room the contents came out of example: bedroom, kitchen, etc.

- o Double check the accuracy of your inventory listing. Ensure all your valuable items are accounted for. Ensure items such as DVDs, CDs, etc are accounted for by quantity…for example, "76 CDs". It is important that you keep an individual list of all titles. You may also attempt to attach this to the packer's inventory sheet or place a copy in the box.

- o Have at least two people present to watch the movers pack your items. Ensure fragile items are properly packed. Ensure items are properly inventoried.

- **Moving in day:**

  - o Ensure at least two people are present. As each box comes into the dwelling, have your copy of the inventory sheet and mark off each box as it comes in. Double check your valuables before you release the movers. Ensure any discrepancies are documented on their forms. Some movers will ask you to leave the paperwork blank or tell you that you have 90 days to write up what is missing….**if it is missing at the time of arrival write it down no if ands, or buts about it**.

  - o Ensure that every damaged or unaccounted for item is recorded on the sheet provided for damaged or missing items/boxes.

  - o Examine all items carefully before signing the paperwork. Be sure that the packers unpack everything you request them to, and take all boxes and packing material with them. If you do not have them unpack boxes they are **not** responsible to return to pick up the boxes and paper. If you desire the movers to take the packing paper and boxes with them and/or have them assembly furniture, **do so before you sign the paperwork!** *If you sign the paperwork and they promise to come back to get the boxes/trash or assemble something...chances are you will not see them again. Because you released them from their obligation, the company saved money and if you complain you legally released them..*

- o Do all of these things in a polite and courteous manner, and do not give the impression that you expect the movers to steal from you.

- o Have food and beverages available for the movers. Kindness goes a long way.

- o Check with your local transportation office to see if you have the option to request your household goods be packed in crates. This way the crates are sealed or nailed shut and your boxes are not simply packed on the back of a moving van. They are more secure.

- o *Make sure that your moving crates are sealed in your presence and you record the serial numbers of the seals. Do not allow the moving company to tell you that your items will be sealed at another location.*

- o Should you have any problems during your *move out day* or your *move in day* call your local transportation office and ask for a quality control representative. Normally they will visit you once during your move out and move in dates.

- For your responsibilities, responsibilities of the packers, and weight limits read DA PAM 55-2.

Money & Moving: Is there any additional pay associated with moving to help defray the expense of moving? Yes, such pay includes:

THE MILITARY SPOUSE

- **Advance pay:** This pay is equal to one month's base pay of the service member. It should be considered a loan and is available at the time of PCS and can be repaid over the period of one year. It is much like an interest free loan. It must be requested, and it is not automatic. It can be obtained prior to departure or upon arrival at the new unit. Unless you are in financial difficulty we recommend that you *do not* take an advance pay because you are simply taking money away from yourself for the next 12 months.

- **Move in allowance:** If moving overseas, you may be eligible for a one time allowance. Overseas, typically unfurnished apartments are just that – unfurnished. No lights, cabinets, sinks, appliances, etc. Ask about this allowance during your in-processing. *Check the Thrift Shop for good deals on furniture and appliance needs.*

- **Dislocation allowance:** The dislocation allowance is equal to 2 months of Basic Allowance for Housing (BAH). Each pay grade has a different rate authorized for BAH. This money is normally given when you out process from your unit and it is not taxable; nor are you required to pay it back.

- **Travel pay:** The service member is authorized travel pay for themselves, their spouse, and dependent children. You can obtain this in an advance payment and receive the balance when you arrive at your new duty station, or you can receive it all at your new duty station.

- **Temporary Lodging Allowance (TLA):** You are normally authorized up to 10 days of TLA. This is a reimbursable allowance that you must apply for. It is not taxable. It is used to help defray the cost of staying in a hotel and eating out while you get settled at your new duty station and while departing your current duty station. See your local finance office for details.

- **Spend your money wisely:** Many military families get in financial difficulty during moves. Keep track of how much you spend and do not use your travel money as vacation money. If you keep careful track of your money you will find that you will probably have more than enough money in your budget when you arrive at your next duty station. **In addition, keep track of all your associated moving costs. Anything above what the military has paid *may* be tax deductible. You must keep accurate records and consult a tax professional.**

Army Regulation 37-104: Read this regulation it explains all pay and financial options available to a service member.

Time For Moving: Each service member is provided approximately 10 days to clear (other branches of the services are provided varying amounts of time) an installation. Some installations differ and provide less days but usually no fewer than 7 days. In addition to this time service members are usually provided the following time:

- **In processing time:** This can range from 3-7 days depending on the unit location, and local policies.

- **Travel time:** Each service member is given a specified number of days to travel from their current duty assignment to their new duty assignment. This usually ranges from 1-3 days but can be more depending on the move. This time is not charged against a service member's normal leave time.

- **Permissive TDY (PTDY):** A service member can request this leave from their departing unit, up to 10 days, for "house hunting" (again other services having different policies) upon arriving at his/her new duty station. Usually the service member must sign in at the gaining installation with the housing office prior to his/her leave ending to begin PTDY.

Ordinary Leave: Service members normally take leave in conjunction with a *Permanent Change of Station (*PCS) move, or in

THE MILITARY SPOUSE

civilian language "HONEY LET'S PACK OUR STUFF IT'S TIME TO MOVE"! A service member earns 2.5 days of leave a month. The normal leave time for a PCS move ranges from 1 week to 60 days depending on the amount of time the service member has earned and the required report date at the next duty station. Leave requests in excess of 30 days must normally be approved by a Commander in the Grade of O-5 or higher. *To obtain more information on leave, Permissive TDY and other special passes for Army Personnel please see the AR 600-8-10. Our sister service spouses should look up their applicable regulation or instruction.*

De-Junking Day: Before you leave, it would be great to get rid of everything you don't need or have not used in the last year. Chances are if you have not used it in the last year you probably won't realistically use the item enough to make it worth moving to the next location. This is a great opportunity to have your children (and the adults) go through toys, clothes, appliances, and others items and set them aside to be sold or given to charity. Currently there are computer programs such as "**It's Deductible**" that you can buy and these type of programs allow you to document items and gives you fair market value of the item to deduct on your taxes based on the condition of the item. Some products even allow you to attach pictures to the file. This helps should the IRS come knocking. Giving to charity is always a good thing…even if you don't have enough to deduct from your taxes. It serves two purposes to give to charity: (1) you get rid of items that are taking up space, and (2) you provide items to needy individuals.

Another option is a yard sale. If you live on base you may need to have approval from the Post Commander to have a yard sale. Some neighborhoods or cities also have restrictions, so do your homework. You may earn a little extra money and what does not sell you can give to charity.

Hitting the Road:

- Plan your route.

- Inform family members of the route you plan to take.

- Make hotel arrangements along the route.

- Break your trip in to manageable legs.

- Have an atlas available with your route well marked. Also, consider using online mapping programs to make distinguishing turns, exits, foods/drink, and rest room areas. If you really want to go all out get a portal Global Positioning System (GPS) for your car. It will talk to you, tell you where to turn, what exit to take, what you can get to eat/drink/availability of restrooms, etc.

- Travel during non peak hours....*especially when traveling thru large cities.*

- Have a bag or cooler with munchies for the road. Include something for everyone.

- Have items to keep children occupied, like road trip games, DVDs, and video games.

- Have emergency equipment available: jumper cables, first aid kit, warning lights, flashlight, etc. Also, check your spare tire.

- Pack the vehicle in a way that limits blind spots.

- Do not drive beyond your capabilities (time, distance, etc).

- Know the weather channels or carry a weather radio.

THE MILITARY SPOUSE

- If traveling in more than one car, have walkie talkies or cell phones for each vehicle.

Types Of Travel: There are two types of travel, concurrent and non-concurrent.

- **Concurrent travel:** Family members can travel with you at the time of your move. More than likely, quarters will be available for your family within 30 days of arrival.

- **Non-concurrent travel:** Your family members cannot accompany you to your new duty station. This normally means quarters are not projected to be immediately available. Your family will be authorized travel once quarters are available. If you receive non-concurrent travel, you can request thru your military personnel office to have your orders changed to concurrent travel. In addition, if your spouse is a local national of the area in which you will be assigned, or if you have friends already in the country willing to allow you to stay with them, this is usually sufficient to receive concurrent travel.

Making A House A Home: Some ideas on how to make your house feel like home are the following:

- Paint the interior walls of the new home, but get approval first if it is government owned or you are renting. Another method of wall decorating is to take a fabric you like cut it in strips so it fits your wall, then soak in liquid starch, wring out excess, and put it on your walls, using a flat piece of wood or other flat surface press out the wrinkles. The result is an inexpensive wall paper that looks great, and best of all you can just peel it off when you move.

- Buy things from the country you are in…when you finally settle down your home will have a small flavor of every country you have traveled to.

- Hang your family photos on the wall, brighten up the house with small flower or wall arrangements, and accent colors with accessories like pillows and throws.

Homeowners Assistance Program (HAP): The military provides assistance for homeowners as a result of:
- Spouses relocating as a result of a service member that die in the line of duty after Sept 11, 2001
- Wounded warriors relocatining for medical treatment or retirement
- Service members forced to relocate as a result of base realignment and closure (BRAC) decisions
- Service members forced to sell their homes as a result of permanent change of station.

If you believe your qualify go to: *hap.usace.army.mil* .

CHAPTER 9
HEY! WHAT ABOUT *MY* CAREER?

Note: (Website use) for more information on obtaining a job, please utilize the website section of this book. It will provide you with useful websites for job searches and other information.

As an old saying goes, when you marry a service member you marry the service and its way of life. Be prepared to change locations on average every 2-5 years. Currently, the military is looking at changing the length of time a service members stay at one location to 5 - 8 years. This effort will dramatically help spouses obtain, maintain and develop their own career. In addition it will provide stability for children attending school. The service member may deploy several times during this period but the family will remain in the same location. *Numerous companies have started programs for military spouses and will try to transfer them to a job at the new duty assignment. We recommend you check with some of the larger retail and home improvement companies. The larger the company, the better opportunity you have of securing a job with them at your new duty station.*

Types Of Government Jobs: Government Schedule offers several options of governmental employment. Most of us are familiar with the category titled GS (Government Service), but other Government Schedule jobs include WG (Wage Grade), and SES (Senior Executive Service) jobs. There are several types of jobs you may be interested in. Some of these include:

- **SES positions:** This service is the top of government service personnel. These individuals administer public programs at the top levels of Federal Government and are primarily managerial and supervisory. Salaries in these positions normally start in the $100,000 range.

- **GS positions:** These positions range from GS-1 to GS 15. These positions have a wide variety of skills associated with them. As a guide, depending on your qualifications (previous work experience and level of education), most entry jobs will start between a GS-3 and GS-5. These jobs normally tend to offer the convenience of predictable schedules, benefits, and the possibility to work modified work schedules. If you meet certain conditions at the time you are changing location, you may be eligible for reinstatement at your next location.

- **WG positions:** These positions are considered blue collar worker positions and could include positions like heavy equipment operator, forklift operator, etc. These jobs usually offer the same benefits as that of a GS worker to include the ability to be reinstated if you meet the requirements.

Note: Keep in mind that government jobs are not limited to jobs on the installation. They can also include jobs with the postal service, the FBI, prison system, or other federal agencies. Jobs in the government system are usually not easily obtainable even at entry level positions.

Types of Non Government Jobs on an Installation:

- **Army Air Force Exchange System (AAFES):** Typically the easiest and most transferable jobs come in the form of working for the Exchange System (Army =Post Exchange, Air Force =Base Exchange, NavEX= Naval Exchange for the Navy and Marines). These jobs tend to offer lower paying jobs (minimum wage or better), positions are normally available with full or part time status, and may even provide benefits and room for career growth. However, work hours tend to be centered on the evenings and weekends. This means that while your family is home, you may be working. Under certain conditions you may have reinstatement rights at your next duty location. These jobs include a variety of skills that include jobs like: cashiers, sales associates, food service personnel, etc. In the AAFES system you have the potential to work in a variety of stores like The PX main store, the Shopette (like a convenience store), Class VI (sells bulk alcoholic beverages, usually combined with a shopette), Food Court or cafeteria personnel, Post Gas Station, Post Theater, and others.

- **Non-Appropriated Fund (NAF) positions:** These positions are somewhat like the positions offered by AAFES in that the skills are normally similar. However, positions in areas like administration, marketing, etc may also be available at your location. Employment may be part time or full time, and benefits may be included for full time employees with the option of reinstatement at the next duty location if certain requirements are met. Pay varies according to grade level (ranges from NAF 1-4) and positions are normally pay banded (meaning pay is set across a range for each level, with pay being decided based on the qualifications of the individual and the profitability of the organization). In addition most NAF organizations are required to turn a profit to stay in business. This means that positions are subject to elimination if the facility or service is not turning a profit. Jobs in the NAF system on an installation may include: Arts and Craft Center, Auto Skills Center, Child Development Centers, Youth Centers or programs, Marketing, Fitness Centers, etc.

Private Industry: Opportunities are usually abound in this arena. Depending on your location, the job market can be very lucrative or almost none existent. Here are some points about employment in private industry:

- **Barriers about private industry:**
    - If it is known that you are a military spouse some employers may hesitate to seriously consider you for a position because they know that your employment is only temporary. From their point of view, they may be wondering why they should invest time and money in

training someone they know will not be able to stay with the organization.

- Some organizations may have an aversion to the military service.

- You can expect questions that include: "When did you arrive in the area? How long do you expect to stay in the area? Do you know when your spouse will be transferred to another location?" You may even be asked inappropriate questions like: "What job does your spouse hold or what is their rank/position?"

- **Positive aspects to working with private industry:**

  - Many employers desire military spouses because they can usually offer part time positions that do not include a benefits package (this saves them money), which also means you may be able to ask for a higher salary. The employers know as a military spouse you do not usually have concerns about health/dental or other insurance requirements, *which saves them money.*

  - Many defense contractors employ retired service members or individuals who have served in the military. This can serve to break down barriers and open up opportunities.

  - If you have a job with a large firm; for example a defense contractor, or large department store or business, you may have the opportunity to move into a position at your next location without loss of benefits or pay.

  - The skills you obtain in industry may assist in making you competitive for government service positions.

- Ensure that the job you accept will not embarrass your spouse or the military or potentially case a perception of conflict of interest.

Home Business: You may have a position or skill that allows you to telecommute or that allows you to operate a home business. Perhaps the most common home business in the military is home childcare. While the income for this type of work can be great, it requires training and certification, inspections and background checks.

If you operate a home business on the installation you will need to check to see if there are any restrictions for operating a home business on the installation.

Temporary Hiring Agencies: Reputable agencies may be able to assist you in getting your foot in the door with large companies. They typically provide assistance in interview techniques, what type of salary to expect, and how you should approach a particular interview. They are usually paid by the company to screen out undesirable candidates and are typically paid by the company for their services if you are hired on a permanent basis. Temporary hiring agencies have an interest in helping you put your best foot forward. Ensure you are working with a **reputable agency**. Check with the Better Business Bureau for the right company to go with..

Volunteering: This is perhaps one of the best ways to learn job skills, get to know people, see how the system works, break down barriers, and to see if you enjoy working in a particular field. In addition, you may be able to volunteer in an organization that will be losing a person in the near future. If you do a good job and have the required skills you may have a better opportunity at the position for the reasons mentioned previously.

If you volunteer, consider the following organizations on post: Army Community Service (or our sister service equivalent), The Red Cross (you can also volunteer with organizations off post), the post vet clinic, any local hospital or other organization that recruits volunteers. The Chamber of Commerce may have a list they can provide. Volunteering provides you:

- Exposure to a potential employer.

- Allows a potential employer the ability to observe your work ethic and performance.

- May provide you the opportunity to learn new skills.

- Add skills and experience to your resume.

- Last but not least, it provides you with the opportunity to give back to your community.

Preparing For A Job: The best way to prepare for a job is to develop a good plan. Here are some suggestions for developing your plan:

- *Step 1: What type of work would you like to obtain a job in?*

    o Remember you never get a 2nd chance to make a 1st impression. If you make a bad one, you may never recover from it, or it may take a long time to recover from it.

    o Always try and be positive about everything. If you are put in a position that requires you to provide negative feedback, try and do it a way that is strictly professional, not condescending, and is not personal in nature. Sometimes you may be required to be the bearer of bad news, but make it as pleasant and positive as possible.

    o Remember that <u>*attitude and tone are everything*</u>. Maintain a positive attitude and an upbeat tone. This is not to say that you have to be a "YES" person or always agree with someone. It simply means that you must find a way to deliver your message in a positive and upbeat manner!

Even the most painful event has a positive side. For example, it maybe a very negative interview for you personally, but the positive side is that it has taught you how to better deal with a situation of this type in the future. Let go of any bitterness, keep things professional. Never let anything become personal.

- Do you have the skills for this type of work?

- Will you need to further your education to get this type of job? If so, develop a plan to further your education.

- Will you need to work to pay for your education or help pay the bills while you go to school? If so, what type of work are you qualified for and would you be interested in performing?

- *Step 2: Prepare your resume*
  - Many first time job seekers fail to capitalize on their skills. For example, a spouse who stays at home and cares for the family may be able to include the following in their resume:

    - Prepares and monitors financial budget.

    - Ability to solve problems and coordinate resources (be prepared to give examples like: helping deployed spouses obtain medical care during emergencies, arranging, organizing child care for a family during a crisis that required several families over the period of say 1 week, etc. The possibilities are endless).

    - Led a Family Support Group for one year:

      - Group consisted of 20 spouses .

- Coordinated all communications for approximately 150 troops' families.
- Provided advice and assistance for families in a variety of crisis situations.
- Planned, organized, and executed 5 fund raising events with 50 volunteers raising over $2,000.
- Developed and audited the organizational budget and all related financial requirements.

- List all awards or honors you have received.

- Include your education level as well as any certifications, college classes, or vocational training you have completed.

- Your skills are limited only by your memory and patience in listing each skill, experience and ability.

- Do not brag or overstate your accomplishments or responsibilities.

- Do not understate your achievements!

- Resume assistance: Once you have an outline of your resume or if you are stuck on how to develop a resume, you can get assistance from the Army Community Service Center. They can provide useful insight into formats, how to structure your resume for a specific job, and what jobs may be available in the local area.

- Buy a book on resume writing: There are several useful writing guides that can help you decide on a format and assist you in developing ideas for content.

THE MILITARY SPOUSE

- o Government resumes versus civilian resumes: Resumes for GS positions tend to be structured different from civilian resumes. The best advice we can give here is to encourage you to talk with several GS employees or managing officials and ask for assistant, advice, and example resumes. You must tailor your resume to fit the specific job you are seeking. The most important thing is to find someone you respect in management and get their advice and assistance in developing your resume.

- *Step 3: Get organized.*

  - o Prepare a 3 ring binder that is organized containing:
    - All your previous evaluations.
    - All your previous awards or items of recognition.
    - A reference list that should contain: name, address, phone number, email address, their relationship to you, how long you have known the person, etc.
    - Letters of recommendation and references.
  - o Know what you will accept as a minimum in terms of salary and benefits. When determining these minimums, be sure to include the following factors:
    - You need to make a profit after all your expenses are paid. It makes no sense to work if it costs you more money to work than to stay home, or if the amount of money you will receive as net pay will not be sufficient compensation. Look at child care expenses, gasoline, and transportation costs, etc.

- How much will come out of your paycheck for Federal and State Taxes? We suggest that you file at the Single and Zero rate. This will help you at income tax time and you will either get a refund or the amount you will have to pay will be smaller because your taxes will be taken out at the single rate which is higher than the married rate.

- Will you have to pay child care? How much?

- What will the cost of gas be?

- Are there any additional costs associated with the job, like parking fees or mass transit tickets?

- *Step 4: Get the word out.*

    o Now you're ready to start applying for positions.

    o Utilize the websites in this book to search for government and other jobs.

    o Look for a reputable temporary agency in your area and leave your resume with them.

    o Speak with your friends and let them know you are looking for a job.

    o While you are looking for a job, consider volunteering in the area you are trying to get a job. It provides exposure and experience.

    o You need all the exposure you can get. Volunteer and work in the community.

- *Step 5: The interview.*

THE MILITARY SPOUSE

- Before the interview, find out everything you can about the company, their mission, process, and the leadership (if possible). Be well informed about them. Let them know you are interested in the company. Have questions ready that relate to their mission. Be prepared to tell them how hiring you can help them.

- Ensure you are dressed appropriately for the interview.

- Be a few minutes early. Do not be late!

- Be prepared for tough questions. For example, let's say you are applying for a position as a receptionist and one of the individuals interviewing you asks: "you receive a call from an upset customer complaining of poor service. The individual is very frustrated. How would handle this situation?"

- Be able to explain why you should be hired over someone else. Your response should not put others down but you could response with something like: "While I am sure the other candidates are qualified I believe I am the best qualified because I am loyal, dependable, willing and eager to learn, etc..."

- Do not let salary be the driving force in the interview. Provide a range depending on the average salary in your area. Use either an hourly rate or annual salary.

- They may ask you for traits you consider to be your stronger points and your weak points. Consider these carefully in advance!

- Be prepared to talk in general about your expectations of hours worked, time off, benefits, etc. This allows the company to think about what they may want to offer you. If you have done your homework you know what the average salary is and have provided them a range in the average or based upon your experience you may decide to up the salary range. Perhaps you don't have the job skills or your skills are not exactly to the specification they are looking for. In this case you may want to come in with a range that is slightly below to just inside the average salary. This method allows the employer room to make you an offer based on your skills and what they can reasonably offer.

- Do not be concrete on responses. You may lock yourself out of the job without even knowing it. For example, let's say one of the individuals interviewing you asks: "This job may require weekend work or hours beyond our normal work day. How do you feel about this?" Your response might be, "I'm flexible and can work around most issues." This response indicates you are willing to work if needed.

- As you close the interview, find out when would be an appropriate time to contact the company regarding the interview to do a follow up.

- Write the individual that conducted the interview a thank you note.

- The interview also provides you an opportunity to get a look at the individuals you may be working with or perhaps working for. This can help you decide if you want a job with the company. Use this time to evaluate the company and decide if you would be happy working in the company as a result of how you were treated or the atmosphere. Remember the interview process gives you a snapshot of the company just as the interview gives the company a snapshot of you. Some areas or questions you may want to look at in this area are:

- How do they treat their employees?

- How professional are they?

- What type of atmosphere did you notice when you entered the company?

- Did the other employees seem happy, were they friendly towards you?

- How were you greeted?

- What was the dress code for the company? (Formal, casual, etc).

○ Consider every interview as the interview for your next job! Do not consider one interview as less important than another. Most of all, understand every interview is a chance for you to better your presentation skills and it exposes you to different styles of interviews.

○ Always send a thank you card or email. It is professional, shows you are sincerely interested, keeps you in the mind of the person who interviewed you, and always end with a statement like: "Looking forward to seeing you again" or "Perhaps we could do lunch at some point in the near future."

- *Step 6: The offer.*

    ○ Be prepared for a job offer at the end of the interview. Chances are this will not happen but you need to be prepared just in case. Remember, while you are being interviewed you are also deciding if this is a company you what to work for. So it is imperative to have an idea prior to your arrival, or at least before agreeing to be employed there.

- o When you get a wage offer you should already know the minimum amount you can accept. Therefore if the offer is below this point see if there is room for discussion or negotiation. Try to raise it to at least your minimum. If they will not meet your minimum requirement, you must decide if you will accept the position anyway.

- o Also understand that if they are not going to have to incur the expense of health, dental, or retirement fund expenses you have just saved them about 21%. Therefore you should have some room to bargain or at least surface the issue that you are not receiving benefits, therefore there should be room for negotiation.

- o If you cannot accept the offer, understand the military and usually the local community is a small world. Turn down the offer in a professional and courteous manner. Do not burn any bridges!

Tips in Looking For a Job:

- Remember that all federal jobs are not on post. Look off post!

- Consider a job with the state or city government.

- It's not just enough to have a good work ethic. Performance is only part of the equation. You must have and project a good image. This means that when people walk away from meeting you, they should walk away with a positive and lasting impression. Next, you need to look at how many people know you. This is directly

THE MILITARY SPOUSE

related to your image. As you come to know more people your exposure grows and so does your image.

- Volunteering is an excellent way to open up your image and exposure to other individuals you would not normally interact with.

- Find a mentor - someone who knows and understands the organization you are interested in. Show them your resume, ask them for recommendations to improve it, ask for guidance, and learn from them.

Education: Education is a must if you desire a career in a specific field or expect to move up in a field. If you do not have a High School diploma, get your GED! If you have not completed any college courses, consider getting a degree. If you have a degree, consider furthering your education. You may also consider correspondence courses, seminars or certifications in a field that interests you.

Your local Education Office can assist you with numerous opportunities that include information on:

- GED completion programs.

- Local education opportunities.

- Scholarship opportunities for military spouses. In addition, many scholarships go unclaimed each year because no one knew about them. The money is available if you are willing to put in the time to research them and do a little homework.

- There are interest free or low interest loans available. Check the internet.

Eventually your hard work and effort will pay off with a rewarding job! Good luck and best wishes!

PATRICIA GERECHT & MARK GERECHT

CHAPTER 10
FAMILY MATTERS
HANDLING DOMESTIC ISSUES

All families will go thru difficulties at times and throughout this book there will be ideas and tips about how to handle some of these events. *However, we must stress we are not legal experts or trained professionals. We are simply providing information for the purpose of education, entertainment, and to provoke thought. If the reader has an issue they believe needs to be addressed, then they need to immediately contact the proper military agency such as: National Military Family Association, Army Emergency Relief, Navy Marine Corps Relief Society, Air Force Aid Society, Coast Guard Mutual Assistance, Army Community Service, and/or the Installation or Base Chapel. If the family situation becomes serious or life threatening, we urge you to contact the military or civilian police and/or military or civilian medical support.*

The military member contends with constant deployments coupled with working days of 12-14 hours and as a result they may bring a certain amount of stress home with them. In addition, a spouse has probably had just the same amount of stress between raising children, getting children off to school, perhaps taking care of the home, and more than likely working a job as well. Stress levels can be significant. If you believe stress is a problem in your home seek counseling and support immediately. Don't let pride get in your way. The less stress at home the better the family becomes and the more children enjoy their parents and being together. You can visit your local ACS, chain of command, or hospital to get assistance with anger management or help in dealing with stress. *<u>Spouse abuse in any fashion is unacceptable and will not be tolerated by the chain of command</u>.* If stress levels are high you may also contact Military One Source for counseling at no charge!

Lautenberg Amendment *(Domestic Violence):* As we begin to explore potential spousal abuse let's look at a law entitled the <u>Lautenberg Amendment</u>. It makes it a felony for all active, Reserve, and National Guard service members convicted of a misdemeanor crime of domestic violence to ship, transport, possess, or receive firearms or ammunition. *You may be asking, "so how does this affect me and my family?" If your spouse is a military member and is convicted of spousal abuse he/she will lose his/her ability to carry a weapon in the military, and in effect, they will be ending their military career.*

It is important for adults to understand the seriousness of this law. Should a false report be rendered and go undetected it is possible the service member could lose his/her career and the family could be without stable income. On the other hand, if this type of behavior is going on it must be reported…it cannot be tolerated! If you sincerely believe an individual is being abused you have the duty to report it. Keep in mind that when police arrive on the scene of a domestic dispute *usually someone is going to jail for an evening.* In some states, both parties go to jail.

The Lautenberg Amendment applies to individuals who have been convicted of spousal abuse. These individuals are non-deployable, and are prohibited from reenlisting. They may extend their time in service for 1 year, which allows the service member to try and expunge the conviction from their records. These service members may also apply for a discharge. *In addition, a summary court martial conviction or non judicial punishment under Article 15 is not considered a misdemeanor conviction.* Therefore, this type of punishment does not invoke the requirement of the amendment. This is very important to understand.

Failing to take proper action to resolve issues between you and your spouse in a responsible manner could result in one or both of you being arrested and potentially the military member being charged under the Lautenberg Amendment. Believe it or not, some spouse's have used this to inadvertently harm a service member's career…only to find out it had a significant impact on the entire family.

THE MILITARY SPOUSE

We want to be clear if matters of spouse abuse or other behavior that is illegal, unethical, or immoral are occurring - report them. There are methods and programs to assist families with these issues. However, if in fact information is falsely reported it can cause even deeper problems between relationships and have severe consequences for the individual making the false report.

Please keep in mind when police or military authorities respond to an incident you have usually lost your ability to control the situation. In these cases the chain of command may separate the parties involved for a period of 72 hours to cool off.

Be smart about conflict resolution. Solve your problems calmly! If emotions are running high, someone should leave the room or the house to allow the situation to cool off until both people can talk reasonably. Take turns talking and listening to each other…otherwise you may find yourself being required to attend training and your problems may become more public than you desire.

Keep Your Private Life Private (Within Reason): Last but not least, keep your personal life private. You should only discuss issues with an individual you can really trust. By talking about your problems openly or with an untrustworthy individual you will open yourself and your family up to significant grief. Rumors will fly, and friendships and relationships can and usually are damaged. The military is a small world and word travels fast…if you are in doubt about talking with someone choose a trusted source or a confidential source like the chaplain or your minister. Sometimes you just need to vent…make sure you vent to the right person…the right person should never be someone in your spouses' chain of command or the spouse of a leader in your spouses' chain of command.

You may also be entitled to certain benefits if you are the victim of a crime. For more information see *your local Legal office or post community service organization. First and Foremost Never* tolerate abuse!

Prenuptial Agreements: When it is time to get married none of us want to think about divorce, let alone believe it will happen to us. Unfortunately in today's society, couples often believe they can trade one problem for another. While we do not personally agree with prenuptial agreements or divorce, we believe you should at least be informed about some of the issues that surround them as they relate to the military. Our best advice is to understand that all of us make mistakes in our lives and together as a team you can work through anything.

- *Why a prenuptial agreement:* Many couples are marrying later in life and may have significant assets and/or children from previous marriages and want to protect their financial well being. These agreements are commonly used to protect financial assets, protect inheritance, and to make prearranged financial agreements. In addition, they may include privileges, division of property, child custody, etc. If you are both young with minimal assets you probably do not need a prenuptial agreement. If however you have a significant amount of assets or the desire to protect an inheritance or children you may need to consider these options.

Divorce: While military legal offices cannot represent you in a divorce, they can assist you in drawing up separation agreements and advise you as to your rights with regard to child support, monetary support, and other entitlements through your divorce process. Keep in mind that legal offices have to prevent conflict of interest. Therefore, if one member of the couple goes to the installation's legal office, the other may have to go to another base to receive advice.

Should the worst happen and a divorce is the route you choose then you should acquire professional legal assistance. Your military attorney can usually provide a list of attorneys for you to choose from. In some cases if the separation or divorce is amicable you may not need separate attorneys. However it would be in your best interest to at least have a disinterested attorney review the agreement to ensure you are receiving a fair settlement. You and your spouse can reduce the cost and emotional strain by reaching a common understanding and minimizing any conflicts.

THE MILITARY SPOUSE

Divorce will include a wide range of emotions. How will you pay the bills, get your new life off the ground, take care of your children, and you will at times be overwhelmed by emotions. Marriage counselors and pastors can be of tremendous help and may be able to assist you in making better or more informed decisions. It is critical that you remain focused on your finances and work to better your situation. Do not feel pressured to make critical decisions or rush your way thru a divorce.

Once the divorce is final you will begin the process of putting your life back together. You will have to make plans and being building a new life. It will be important emotionally to move on with your life and understand that it is only a temporary setback and you will overcome this event and good days are ahead. You simply need to make wise and healthy choices. Make sure that insurance policies are reviewed and updated prior to the divorce settlement. Make a budget, set goals, and establish an emergency fund to begin to build your life anew. Remember, you will often experience the feeling of two steps forward and one step back…but you are making progress. Avoid new romantic relationships right after a divorce.

Money and Marriage: Money is perhaps one of the leading causes of arguments among couples. You must not allow money or material possessions to dictate your relationship. Remember you are in this together. Whether you have one or two paychecks, you are a team, and the finances need to be managed as such. You should sit down and come up with a budget that includes bills, savings, and spending plans. Agree to make a commitment to each other that you will abide by this agreement or adjust it as necessary.

PATRICIA GERECHT & MARK GERECHT

CHAPTER 11
PREPARING FOR THE FUTURE

As young couples, we expect that poor health and death will come, but not until a much later stage in life. We tend to ignore the requirements to plan for the death or the significant injury of a loved one. The most important thing we can do is make a plan for an unfortunate incident and know our benefits. We urge you use this chapter to assist you in making necessary/prudent decisions and as a method to know and understand your benefits.

When a tragic event occurs, our minds are usually overwhelmed by the situation and further burdened by the difficult decisions we must make. My husband has had the unfortunate opportunity to be a Casualty Assistance Officer (CAO). You may be familiar with a similar term used by our sister services Casualty Assistance Representatives (CAR) for several service members. In 2 out of 3 cases, my husband returned home after his initial meeting with the spouse in somewhat of a somber mood. He could not believe that the couple had not made, or had only made minimal arrangements for the future of the family in the event of a death. After his first duty as a CAO officer, we began to plan for the future, even though we hoped such tragedy would not come in the near future. We now have peace of mind knowing that most of the major decisions have already been made. We strongly encourage you and your spouse to sit down and plan for unforeseen events. It will give your family peace of mind and help them during difficult times.

As you begin to make decisions do not focus just on the military member and the present situation, look into the future as best you can. This means looking situations like:

- Your first step should be to find a military lawyer, a certified financial planner, and an insurance agent you trust. Remember the last two are in business to make money off of you, so ensure that they have your best interest at hand, and not their pockets.

- How many children do you plan to have or do you have?

- What will it take financially to meet your child's/children's immediate needs for food, clothing, shelter, and education?

- What will your needs be 10, 15, 20, years from now?

- What happens if the non military spouse passes on:

    o Will the military member continue to serve in the armed services?

    o If the non military spouse was working, how will you replace their loss of income?

    o How will the military member pay for the increased cost of childcare?

The next several pages will discuss items we know are important and you should consider in your planning process. *Please keep in mind the information provided is to educate and provoke thought. You will need to seek expert legal advice and possibly the advice of a sound financial planner you trust in order to properly plan your desires. Your local JAG office can provide assistance in most of these issues.*

Wills: First and foremost **both** you and your spouse need to prepare a will. This is a critical step and needs to be well thought out. I have been told that a will prepared by the military is good in all 50 states. However, I would encourage you to change your will after each move, and also review it and make changes to it any time you have a significant change in your life; such as the birth of a child or a significant increase in assets. Ensure that you also designate the individual or individuals that will take on the responsibility of raising your minor children if both of you are deceased. Ensure that these individuals are willing to accept this huge responsibility. Once your will is complete place one copy of it in a safety deposit box and provide at least two copies to other individuals you trust. In addition, ensure a trusted person knows the location of the key to your safety deposit box and is able to gain access to your box in the event of your death.

Appointing An Executor Of Your Estate: It is critical that you designate someone as the executor of your estate. It is important that this person be trustworthy and fully understands your desires and wishes. Normally spouses will elect each other as the executor, but what happens if a tragic accident occurs that takes both of your lives or incapacitates both of you? The individual you appoint needs to be someone you absolutely trust to look after the best interest of your children and the distribution of assets. We would encourage you to appoint two individuals as your executors, a primary and an alternate. This allows you flexibility in the event the primary cannot perform the duties.

Notarized Letter of Instruction: Next, we strongly suggest that you prepare a letter of instruction to the executor stating your wishes and desires. The reason for the letter is that if you direct things to be done in your will the executor is bound by these directions and is afforded little or no latitude. If however, you put your desires and instructions in a letter to the executor they have the ability to be flexible in the execution of your desires and wishes. You and your spouse must determine how much flexibility you want to provide the executor of your estate and/or the guardian of your children. See your local legal assistance office for assistance in this matter.

The executor's letter should outline all your wishes and provide all necessary information for the executor to quickly determine your assets, debts, and spell out your desires for your children and their future. In our **opinion** the letter should contain things like:

- A listing of all financial information such as:

- All bank account numbers along with contact numbers and a copy of a bank statement (checking/savings, etc.).

- All investment accounts, with account numbers, and a copy of the investment account statement, with contact numbers.

- All insurance policies both military and civilian for all members of the family, a contact number, and a copy of the front page of the policy.

- All bonds with their locations and the approximate value, type of bonds, contact numbers.

- Any stock or trading accounts, account numbers and points of contact.

- Include papers for closing on real estate, deeds to property, car titles, etc.

- A listing of all debts such as:

  - Credit cards, a point of contact, the credit card account number, and a recent statement of the credit card.

  - Listing of debts owed and points of contact for each debt. For example: home mortgage, car loan, and utility accounts (water, gas, electric, sewage, trash, phone, etc).

- A list of the individuals who have agreed (preferably in writing) to take custody of your child/children in the event of your death or incapacitation. We strongly suggest you select a primary and an alternate custodian, and be sure you have checked with these individuals and that they agree to take on this responsibility.

- How assets will be distributed:

- How is money to be maintained if your child/children are minors? For example, will it be put in a trust fund, bank account, or will it be invested? (If it is to be invested, how is it to be invested? In an aggressive risky venture, or in a safe and secure instrument, or a will it be invested across a wide range of investment instruments so that it is a balanced portfolio?)

- Is there a trust fund for your children? It is possible to establish a trust fund now for your children.

- How will your child/children receive the assets? Will they receive them at age 18 or 21? Will they get the assets in a lump sum or will it be distributed at certain times, in a specified amount until they reach a certain age?

- How much money will you allow the custodian of your child/children to withdraw for clothing, food, school tuition (if children are attending private school), and other expenses?

- How will your assets left to your children be audited to ensure they are being utilized in accordance with your desires? Usually an annual audit is sufficient. This is not to say that the person you entrust your with your estate will steal from your children but you need to have a cross check because individuals do not always manage money correctly, and yes believe it or not, money does have the potential to change people. Therefore, we cannot stress enough the importance of having a cross check or balance to the system. Every dollar distributed from a trust fund or other instrument designated to take care of your children needs to be accounted for.

- It would, in our opinion, be appropriate to designate a specific sum of money to be paid to the custodian of your children on an annual basis for keeping the books, arranging for the audit, and other miscellaneous expenses for raising your children.

Living Will: This document should be prepared by each adult and should provide clear guidance on what life saving and life support measures you wish to be utilized in the event you cannot make medical decisions for yourself. It can state that you do not wish to be kept alive by artificial means for a prolonged period of time. These documents can save your family extensive heartache and legal expenses. By making your desires known in writing, ahead of time, there can be no question of your desires should an unfortunate event arise. You can obtain these at no charge from most military legal offices.

Death Benefits for An Active Duty Member: There are numerous benefits available to service members that die on active duty. It is best to be familiar with these benefits prior to a death. Typically when a tragic event occurs the spouse has so much going on that they do not even have time to begin thinking about the benefits to which they may be entitled. A Casualty Assistance Officer (CAO) is assigned to each active duty case for this purpose.

A spouse may request assistance from the local casualty assistance office if their loved one was a **retiree or veteran of military service**. The CAO can help with required paperwork but are not trained experts in benefits. Therefore it is imperative you become familiar with these benefits or have a financial planner who is. There are classes offered at many military installations, and we recommend you take such classes long before you anticipate you need it.

We will attempt to provide you an overview of the benefits you may be entitled to. *However it is important to remember we are not experts and each case is different. You should seek advice from the local military legal office, the Veterans Administration and the local Casualty Assistance Office.* Please keep in mind that few things happen quickly in the world of benefits. Before we begin to discuss potential benefits here are some suggestions we believe you should consider.

THE MILITARY SPOUSE

Getting Organized:

- Use a 3 ring binder to organize the following information:

    - Get copies of all paperwork you fill out and sign.

    - Get the name of the agency you are speaking to.

    - Get the name of the person you spoke with.

    - Try to get direct numbers to the person you spoke with. If possible, avoid the automated phone lines.

    - Make a summary of the conversation to include:

        - Date and time of the conversation.
        - Person you spoke with facts about the conversation.
        - Request a date to follow up on the situation.

    - Always ask how long the waiting time is to receive a response or benefit.

    - Ask what paperwork you may be asked to provide and how/where to get copies or originals if needed.

    - Ask when would be a good time to follow up with another phone call.

    - Read everything before you sign it. Your (Casualty Assistance Officer) CAO should be able to assist you in this area. Most CAO's will be empathic to your current situation and will want to take care of you as they would want their family provided for in a similar situation.

Potential Benefits:

We made every effort to compile what we believe is a useful listing of military benefits you may be entitled to. However benefits are consistently changing. Your CAO, Local Veterans Administration, Social Security Office, or local Casualty Assistance Office can provide up to date information.

We hope the information provided is helpful and informative. If you should come across a benefit that we have missed or has been discontinued we would greatly appreciate you notifying us so that we can provide the best possible information to our readers.

We hope that you never have to use this information. It is provided for your benefit and to help you help those around you who may be experiencing a tragic event in their life. We are all in this together and the more we do for each other the stronger we become as a team.

Stoppage of Active Duty Pay/Benefits:

Active Duty Pay and Benefits Stop: at the time of death. This means that a service member will receive only the pay and allowances he/she was entitled to at the time of death. Pay will not continue beyond the date of death. The military has two methods that help to reduce financial stress on families during a death, and they are:

- Service member Group Life Insurance (SGLI).

- Death Gratuity Payment. The death gratuity payment is meant to cushion the loss of income until eligibility for other benefits can be determined or activated. Spouses are encouraged to utilize this money sparingly. This money is normally paid within days of the death, and the CAO can help you in this request. More detailed explanation follows.

THE MILITARY SPOUSE

Service Members Group Life Insurance (SGLI): Is a program of low cost group life insurance for service members on active duty, Reservists, members of the Commissioned Corps of the National Oceanic and Atmospheric Administration and the Public Health Service, cadets and midshipmen of the four service academies, and members of the Reserve Officer Training Corps. SGLI coverage is available in $10,000 increments up to the maximum of $400,000. If a service member initially turns down all coverage under SGLI, they may become ineligible for future coverage. We recommend you do not turn it down. SGLI is also available for a specified period of time after separation or retirement from active duty. After this specified period of time service members can convert to Veterans Group Life Insurance (VGLI), however, it is best to check with your financial planner, as more cost effective methods may be available to you. Should an active duty death occur, you will receive assistance immediately from your CAO in filling out this paperwork. The Casualty Assistance Officer (CAO) will then take the paperwork to the local Casualty Assistance Office so that it can be forwarded to the proper offices for processing. Ensure the CAO provides you with a copy of the completed paperwork.

Traumatic Service Members' Group Life Insurance (TSGLI): Army service members who incur a traumatic injury may receive special financial assistance. The purpose is to assist service members and their family members during the extensive recovery and rehabilitation process. Currently this option is available for service members that receive a traumatic injury in support of Operation Iraqi Freedom and Operation Enduring Freedom. Additional information on this benefit can be obtained by calling 1-800-237-1336. The web address is www.aw2.army.mil/TSGLI. Claims can be mailed to: Department of the Army Traumatic SGLI (TSGLI), 200 Stovall St. Alexandria, Va. 22332-0470. TSGLI covers a range of traumatic injuries including but not limited to: total and permanent loss of sight in one or both eyes, loss of hand or foot by severance at or above the wrist or ankle, total and permanent loss of hearing in one or both ears, loss of thumb and index finger of the same hand by severance at or above the metacarpophalangeal joints, quadriplegia, paraplegia, or hemipliega; 3rd degree or worse burns covering 30 % of the body or face and coma or the inability to carry out two of the six activities of daily living due to brain injury.

Family Service Members' Group Life Insurance (FSGLI): Is a program extended to the spouses and dependent children of members insured under the SGLI program. FSGLI provides up to a maximum of $100,000 of insurance coverage for spouses, not to exceed the amount of SGLI the insured member has in force and $10,000 for dependent children. Spousal coverage is issued in increments of $10,000.

Death Gratuity Payment: Next of kin members are given the death gratuity upon the death of an armed service member. The death gratuity payment is tax free and is paid to the next of kin for the following armed service members:

- *An active duty* member or while performing authorized travel to or from active duty; a *Reserve* member of an armed force who dies while on inactive duty training (with exceptions); any Reserve member of an armed force who assumed an obligation to perform active duty for training, or inactive duty training (with exceptions) and who dies while traveling directly to or from that active duty for training or inactive duty training;

- **Any member of a Reserve officers' training corps** who dies while performing annual training duty under orders for a period of more than 13 days, or while performing authorized travel to or from that annual training duty; or any applicant for membership in a reserve officers' training corps who dies while attending field training or a practice cruise or while performing authorized travel to or from the place where the training or cruise is conducted; or a person who dies while traveling to or from or while at a place for final acceptance, or for entry upon active duty (other than for training), in an armed force, who has been ordered or directed to go to that place, and who has been provisionally accepted for that duty; or has been selected for service in that armed force. This

THE MILITARY SPOUSE

check is usually delivered by the CAO. Ensure you request a copy of all paperwork.

Death and Burial: The Department of Veterans Affairs (VA) provides death and burial services for ***eligible active duty, Reserve, and veteran members***. Burial benefits available include: a gravesite in any of the 120 national cemeteries with available space, opening and closing of the grave, perpetual care, a government headstone or marker, a burial flag, and a Presidential Memorial Certificate at no cost to the family. Reimbursement payments are also available for transport of remains, as well as a burial allowance. If preferred, cremated remains are buried in national cemeteries in the same manner and with the same honors as casketed remains.

- **Eligibility:** Generally, service members who die while on active duty and veterans discharged under conditions other than dishonorable are eligible for burial in a VA national cemetery. Reservists and National Guard members are eligible if they were entitled to retired pay at the time of death, or would have been entitled had they not been under the age of 60.

- **Burial of spouses and dependents :**
    - The spouse or un-remarried surviving spouse of an eligible person, even if that person is not buried or memorialized in a national cemetery, is eligible for interment in a national cemetery. In addition, the spouse of a member of the Armed Forces of the United States lost or buried at sea, or officially determined to be permanently absent in a status of missing or missing in action, or whose remains have been donated to science or cremated and the ashes scattered is also eligible for burial.

    - The surviving spouse of an eligible decedent who remarries an ineligible individual and whose remarriage is void, terminated by the ineligible individual's death, or dissolved by annulment or divorce is eligible for burial in a national cemetery. The surviving spouse of an eligible decedent who remarries an eligible person retains his or her eligibility for burial in a national cemetery.

- **Minor children:** For purpose of burial in a national cemetery, a minor child is a person who is unmarried and is under the age of 21 years; or, who is under 23 years of age and pursuing a course of instruction at an approved educational institution, or an unmarried adult child of an eligible person if the child is physically or mentally disabled and incapable of self-support before reaching the age of 21 years. Proper supportive documentation must be provided, and should be kept with your important papers.

- **Persons not eligible for burial in a National Cemetery:**

  - **Remarried surviving spouses married to a non-veteran:** A surviving spouse of an eligible decedent who marries an ineligible individual and predeceases that individual. _Pertains to the non serving spouse._

  - **Former spouses:** A former spouse of an eligible individual whose marriage to that individual has been terminated by annulment or divorce, if not otherwise eligible.

  - **Other family members:** Extended family members of an eligible person.

  - **Disqualifying conditions of discharge:** A person whose only separation from the armed forces was under dishonorable conditions or whose character of service results in a bar to veterans benefits.

THE MILITARY SPOUSE

- **Discharge from draft:** A person who was ordered to report to an induction station, but was not actually inducted into military service.

- **Persons found guilty of a capital crime:** Under 38 U.S.C. § 2411, interment or memorialization in a VA cemetery or in Arlington National Cemetery is prohibited if a person is convicted of a federal capital crime and sentenced to death or life imprisonment, or is convicted of a state capital crime, and sentenced to death or life imprisonment without parole. Federal officials are authorized to deny burial in veteran cemeteries to persons who are shown by clear and convincing evidence to have committed a federal or state capital crime but were not convicted of such crime because of flight to avoid prosecution or by death prior to trial.

- **Subversive activities:** Any person convicted of subversive activities after September 1, 1959, shall have no right to burial in a national cemetery from and after the date of commission of such offense, based on periods of active military service commencing before the date of the commission of such offense, nor shall another person be entitled to burial on account of such an individual. Eligibility will be reinstated if the President of the United States grants a pardon.

- **Active or inactive duty for training:** A person whose only service is active duty for training or inactive duty training in the National Guard or Reserve Component, unless the individual meets the eligibility criteria.

- **Other groups:** Members of groups whose service has been determined by the Secretary of the Air Force under the provisions of Public Law 95-202 as not warranting entitlement to benefits administered by the Secretary of Veterans Affairs.

Health Benefits:

- **TRICARE:** Surviving family members of deceased service members will continue to receive benefits under the TRICARE system as follows:

    o Surviving spouses continue under the same coverage for one year from the death of the service member. After one year, the spouse may pay an annual membership fee equal to that paid by retirees to enroll (or re-enroll) in TRICARE Prime and must pay the cost shares and deductibles applicable to retirees and their families for those who choose the TRICARE Standard or Extra options.

    o Such coverage will continue until the surviving spouse remarries or reaches age 65 (when Medicare coverage begins.

    o Surviving children continue under the same coverage until age 21 or until age 23 if enrolled full time school.

You may contact a Health Benefit Advisor (HBA) near you for more information. You may locate your health benefit advisor by using the internet or by calling the TRICARE number for your region.

- **TRICARE Retiree Dental Plan (TRDP):** The TRDP which offers basic preventive and restorative dental care via civilian dentists is available, provided the following conditions are met:

    o The sponsor's death must have occurred while on active duty in excess of 30 days.

    o Family members must not be eligible, for dental benefits under the TRICARE Family Member Dental Plan.

THE MILITARY SPOUSE

The TRDP offers continuous open enrollment. Initial enrollment is for at least 24 months. After the first 24 month period, enrollees may choose to stay enrolled on a month-to-month basis. Enrollees who disenroll at any time, regardless of the reason, will be subject to a one-year lockout period. Additional information and enrollment forms are available at the following addresses and telephone numbers:

- **Customer Service:** Post Office Box 537007, Sacramento, CA 95853-7007 PH: (888) 336-3260.

- **Enrollment:** Post Office Box 537008, Sacramento, CA 95853-7008 PH: (888) 838-8737.

- *Please keep in mind phone numbers and addresses may change so be sure to confirm this information by utilizing the internet or by contacting your local TRICARE service center.*

Basic Allowance For Housing: The spouse and children (including children from a previous marriage) of a deceased service member living in government quarters are entitled to either remain in government housing for 180 days, or to relocate to private quarters and receive a 180-day Basic Allowance for Housing (BAH) or Overseas Housing Allowance (OHA) as appropriate. Exception to this policy may be granted on a case by case basis by the commander who has the overall responsibility for housing. To receive this allowance for private quarters, the service member must have been eligible to receive those allowances for his or her dependents at the time of death. Note that the entitlement is 180 days, which may be any combination of use of government quarters and or allowances for private quarters. Housing benefits will generally be finalized within 7-14 days of the notification of next of kin.

Federal Employment: Surviving spouses who have not remarried, and certain mothers of deceased members, who served during a war period, are entitled to an additional ten points to their earned rating on the civil service examination. Other benefits with respect to appointment and retention are also available. Information concerning preference eligibility may be obtained from the Office of Personnel Management, State Employment Office, or your local post office.

State Benefits: Many states provide benefits for survivors of veterans such as educational assistance, land settlement preference, civil service preference, tax and license fee exemptions, loans, relief and rehabilitation, employment assistance and bonuses. State Veterans Commissions *(found in your local phone book)* usually supervise these programs and may be contacted for additional information.

Unpaid Compensation: The designated beneficiary will receive any unpaid compensation due the service member on date of death. If no beneficiary was designated, then the recipient will be the surviving spouse. If there is no spouse, then any surviving children or their descendants will receive the funds in equal shares. If there are no children, then the parents of the service member will receive the funds. If there are no parents, then the funds will be distributed either to the person appointed to represent the member's estate or, if no representative was appointed then according to the state probate laws governing the service member's estate.

Complete Standard Form 1174, which is an application to receive the remaining money in the service member's account. The (Casualty Assistance Center Office) CACO will send the paperwork to DFAS and the branch Personnel Office. These claims are usually settled within 60-90 days of the service member's death, and may include pay and allowances accumulated up to the date of death (less any indebtedness to the Government), as well as any unused leave due on the date of death.

Uniformed Services Identification And Privilege Card (DD Form 1173) *(Also known as your ID Card):* The Uniformed Services Identification and Privilege Card identifies the holder as an authorized patron for privileges indicated on the card. Member's dependents over the age of 10 must have a card to gain access to facilities such as the commissary and exchange, or to obtain medical care at a government facility or through a civilian care facility, base theater privileges and so forth. *We highly recommend that you check the expiration date of the ID*

THE MILITARY SPOUSE

Card at least twice a year (for example: your birthday and your anniversary) and renew the card at least 2 weeks prior to the expiration date. It is one of your most valuable documents - guard it closely.

As the surviving dependent of a deceased member your present card expires of the date of the member's death. You must renew this card within 30 days of the member's death in order to continue to have access to the aforementioned privileges. Your CAO will make arrangements for you to receive a new card and will accompany you to the nearest Real-Time Automated Personnel Identification System (RAPIDS) site or other military installation authorized to issue ID cards. You should take the old ID card along with a copy of the DD Form 1300 to the issuing office. You may use your old card for identification until a card is obtained.

Victim Assistance Program: If the death is a result of criminal activity and falls within the purview of the Victim's Rights and Restitution Act of 1990, survivors or dependants of those who died may receive state-sponsored benefits in the form of financial assistance, such as a death gratuity or a loan program, counseling services and other forms of assistance.

The act also provides that the survivors may receive information regarding any criminal investigation, prosecution, incarceration, clemency actions and parole of the person(s) responsible for the death. This includes providing input to the criminal justice system regarding the impact of the crime. Pursuant to this legislation, the Department of Defense has established Victim and Witness Assistance Procedures which are primarily intended to assist victims or their survivors in availing themselves of victim's rights within the military justice system. These procedures also provide a means for survivors to apply for and take advantage of those benefits, which are offered, in every state, in cases which are handled, in civilian jurisdictions. Your CAO will be able to get answers to any questions you may have regarding this program if the military member died as a result of criminal activity.

PATRICIA GERECHT & MARK GERECHT

Survivor Benefit Plan (SBP): SBP is a monthly annuity paid by the military to the surviving spouse or, in some cases, eligible children, of a member who dies on active duty. The initial annuity paid to a surviving spouse is equal to 55 percent of the retired pay to which the member would have been entitled based upon years of active service if retired on the date of death (if the member was retirement-eligible). The annuity is reduced by the amount of the monthly Dependency and Indemnity Compensation (DIC) (*Also see paragraph entitled Dependency and Indemnity Compensation Offset*) payment awarded and paid to the surviving spouse by the Department of VA. When the surviving spouse reaches age 62, the annuity is reduced to 35 percent. The annuity is paid until the spouse dies, but is suspended upon remarriage before age 55. The annuity to a surviving spouse may be reinstated (upon request) if the subsequent marriage ends in death or divorce. The annuitant must send a certified copy of the divorce decree or death certificate to DFAS-DE to reinstate the annuity. If a second SBP benefit resulted from the remarriage, the surviving spouse must elect which of the two SBP benefits to receive. Should the surviving spouse remarry at age 55 or older, the annuitant will continue to receive the monthly annuity. The surviving spouse must notify DFAS-DE/FRB, 6760 E. Irvington Place, Denver CO 80279-6000, of any changes in marital status. Detailed information will be provided by your CAR and the DFAS-DE Center.

Reserve Component Survivor Benefit Plan (RCSBP): This is a monthly annuity paid by the military to the surviving spouse or, in some cases, eligible children, of a Reserve Component member who dies and has completed the satisfactory years of service that qualified the member for retired pay at age 60. The member must have made an election within 90 days of notification of eligibility to participate in the program. Members on an Active Guard/Reserve 10211 (officer) or 12310 (enlisted) tours are eligible to participate in the plan. Coverage is not automatic unless the member dies before the 90 day period established by law. The initial annuity paid to a surviving spouse is equal to 55 percent of the retired pay to which the member would have been entitled at age 60, reduced by the Reserve Portion Cost.

THE MILITARY SPOUSE

- **SBP and RCSBP factors:** Should the surviving spouse remarry before age 55, the annuity is paid in equal shares to eligible children under age 18, or under age 22 if a full-time student, unless handicapped. A child disabled before age 18, or before age 22 if a full-time student when the disability occurred, is an eligible beneficiary so long as the disability exists and the child remains incapable of self-support. The coverage stops when there are no eligible children. A dependent child may be an adopted child, stepchild, grandchild, foster child, or recognized natural child who lived with the member in a regular parent-child relationship.. DFAS-DE reinstates a child's annuity when a child between the ages of 18 and 22 re-enters school on a full-time basis, or a disabling condition recurs making the child incapable of self-support. Marriage at any age terminates a child's eligibility. The monthly annuity for children is 55 percent and is not reduced by DIC or when a disabled child attains age 62. *Survivor annuities are taxable income.* You will receive a tax statement from the Defense Finance and Accounting Service at the end of the year. The statement will show the full amount of the annuity payments you received and the total amount of tax withheld during the year.

Dependency and Indemnity Compensation (DIC) Offset: The Defense Finance and Accounting Service reduces a surviving spouse's annuity by the amount of DIC the VA awards and pays the surviving spouse. The SBP annuity is not reduced by the amount of a child's DIC entitlement. The claim forms required to apply for this benefit are: DD Form 2656-4 (this form is not available electronically), TD-Form W-4P, *Withholding Certificate for Pension or Annuity Payments*, (available from the Post Office or IRS), and SF 1199A, *Direct Deposit Sign-Up Form*. The Defense Finance and Accounting Service may require additional documents in order to establish an annuity (i.e., Representative Payee documentation; school certification; physician's statement for disabled child over age 18).

- **Dependency and Indemnity Compensation (DIC):** The DIC payments may be authorized for surviving spouses who have not remarried, unmarried children under age 18, disabled children, children between the age of 18 and 23 if attending a VA-approved school, and low-income parents of Service members who die from a disease or injury incurred or aggravated while on active duty or active duty for training, an injury incurred or aggravated in line of duty while on inactive duty training, or a disability compensable by the Veterans' Affairs.

DIC paid to a surviving spouse is not based on the member's military pay grade. The amount paid for a spouse with one or more children of the deceased is increased for each child. The amount of the DIC payment for parents vary according to the number of parents, the amount of their individual or combined total annual income, and whether they live together or if remarried, living with a spouse. The surviving spouse and parents who receive DIC may be granted a special allowance for aid and attendance if a patient is in a nursing home, disabled, or blind and needs or requires the regular aid and attendance of another person. If they are not so disabled as to require the regular aid and attendance of another person but who, due to disability, are permanently housebound, they may be granted additional special allowances. DIC payments to a surviving spouse are payable for life, as long as the spouse does not remarry. *Should the surviving spouse remarry, payments are terminated for life.* Your Casualty Assistant Representative (CAR) or the nearest VA office will explain the benefit to you, the amounts that can be paid, and help you complete the required claim forms.

The claim form when applying for this benefit is VA Form 21-534, *Application for Dependency and Indemnity Compensation or Death Pension Accrued Benefits by Surviving Spouse or Child*, or VA Form 21-535, *Application for Dependency and Indemnity Compensation by Parent(s)*.

- **Denial of claim for DIC:** If the VA denies your claim for DIC benefits you may file an appeal with the Board of Veterans' Appeals. The appeal must be filed within one year from the date of the notification of a VA decision to file an appeal. The first step

THE MILITARY SPOUSE

in the appeal process is for you to file a written notice of disagreement with the VA regional office that made the decision. The address or phone number should be on the letter of denial. You may also contact local veteran's groups to obtain assistance in your appeal process. This is a written statement that you disagree with the VA's decision. Following receipt of the written notice, the VA will furnish you a "Statement of the Case" describing what facts, laws and regulations were used in deciding the case. To complete the request for appeal, you must file a "Substantive Appeal" within 60 days of the mailing of the Statement of Case, or within one year from the date the VA mailed its decision, whichever period ends later. Your CAR or the nearest VA office will help you file a written notice of disagreement with the VARO (Veteran Affairs Regional Office) that made the decision.

Nonservice-Connected Death Pension:. If the VARO determines that you are not eligible for DIC, you may be eligible to apply for a non service-connected death pension. Surviving spouses and unmarried children under age 18, age 23 if attending a VA-approved school, of deceased members with wartime service may be eligible for this pension if they meet income limitations prescribed by law. Qualifying children who become incapable of self-support because of a disability before age 18 may be eligible for a pension as long as the condition exists, unless the child marries or the child's income exceeds the income limit (contact your local VA office to find out what the limits are or utilize the VA website). The rate of pension depends on the amount of income the surviving spouse or child receives from other sources. A pension is not payable to those whose estates are so large that it is reasonable to assume the estate will maintain them financially. Eligible survivors should make application through the local VA office. The VA will determine your eligibility.

Educational Benefits and Assistance:

- **Educational benefits:** Educational assistance benefits are available to spouses who have not remarried and children of members who died from a service-connected injury or illness.

163

Benefits may be awarded for pursuit of associate, bachelor or graduate degrees at colleges and universities, including independent study, cooperative training and study abroad programs. Courses leading to a certificate or diploma from business, technical or vocational schools also may be taken. Benefits may be awarded for apprenticeships, on-the-job training programs and farm cooperative courses. Benefits for correspondence courses under certain conditions are available to spouses only. Secondary-school programs may be pursued if the individual is not a high-school graduate. An individual with a deficiency in a subject may receive tutorial assistance benefits if enrolled half-time or more. Deficiency, refresher and other training also may be available. Eligible persons may receive educational assistance for full-time training for up to 45 months or the equivalent in part-time training. Schooling must be in VA-approved schools and colleges. Payments to a spouse end 10 years from the date the individual is found eligible or from the member's date of the death. The VA may grant an extension. In addition to the Dependents Educational Assistance program, various programs are available to help children reach their education goals. For more information, contact the nearest VA office.

- **Scholarship assistance:** For dependent survivors of deceased members is provided by many schools, colleges, special scholarship funds, and by state laws. While such assistance is usually provided only for persons needing financial assistance, some aid may be furnished regardless of need. This is particularly true of state benefits. Additional information on this subject may be obtained from the VA, your local state college board, or by doing an internet scholarship/or interest free loan search.

- **Montgomery GI Bill death benefit:** The VA will pay a special Montgomery GI Bill death benefit to a designated survivor in the event of the service-connected death of an individual while on active duty. The deceased must either have been entitled to

THE MILITARY SPOUSE

educational assistance under the <u>Montgomery GI Bill program</u>, or a participant in the program who would have been so entitled but for the high school diploma or length of service requirement. The amount paid will be equal to the deceased member's actual military pay reduction less any educational benefits paid. If you are eligible to receive the death benefit, submit a letter, along with proof of relationship and a copy of the <u>DD Form 1300</u>, *Report of Casualty*, to the appropriate VA Regional Office. The death benefit is made in "by-law" fashion to the spouse, children, and parents, and will not be paid to anyone else in the "by-law" chain. We encourage you to use all your GI Bill benefits.

- **Scholarship information:** Many states, universities, and other groups sponsor scholarship programs for the children of deceased service members, particularly those with wartime service. Contact your high school guidance counselor, local library, or internet for further information.

Social Security:

- **Social Security payments:** Social Security monthly benefits are paid to a spouse or a divorced spouse, age 60 or over; a spouse or divorced spouse regardless of age with children of the decedent under age 16 or disabled in their care and meeting social security requirements. A divorced spouse must have been married to the service member at least 10 years. Monthly payments are also paid to children until age 18 or 19 if a full-time student at a primary or secondary school, or age 18 or older and disabled before age 18. Spouses waiting until age 65 to apply for Social Security receive maximum benefits. However, they can receive reduced Social Security payments between ages 60 and 65. Dependent parents are eligible for benefits at age 62 if they were more than 50 percent dependent on the deceased service member for their support. The amount paid can only be determined by the Social Security Administration, which has a record of the wages earned by the member during the period of both military and civilian employment under the Social Security Program. To receive this benefit, eligible survivors should make application through the nearest Social Security office. They will explain the benefit, determine your eligibility, the amounts that can be paid, and help you complete the required claim forms. You should apply early, as the law generally permits retroactive payments of 12 months.

- **Social Security lump sum death payment**: Any benefits you may receive from the Social Security Administration (SSA) are administered by that agency independent of any benefits you receive through the military. You should contact the SSA as soon as possible after the service member's death so that your long term benefits can start as soon as possible. Within 30-90 days, SSA will pay to a surviving spouse or children a $255 lump sum death payment and will provide other monthly benefits to surviving family members. The family member is defined as the surviving spouse living with the member at the time of death. Separation because of military service is considered living together. If there is no surviving spouse, it is paid to the oldest child who was eligible for or entitled to Social Security benefits for the month of death, based upon the deceased member's earnings. No other survivors are entitled to this benefit. This benefit is paid regardless if burial, funeral, or memorial benefits were paid by the military. To receive this benefit, eligible survivors must make application through the nearest Social Security office. They will explain the benefit, determine your eligibility, the amount that can be paid, and help you complete the required claim forms. The amount of those benefits depends on how long the service member worked and contributed through Federal Insurance Contributions Act (FICA) payroll deductions. You may also contact the SSA for more information about this benefit at 1-800-772-1213. SSA claims are usually settled within 60-90 days from the date the SSA receives the claim.

THE MILITARY SPOUSE

Commissary Privileges: Subject to the Installation Commander's determination of availability, the unmarried surviving spouse is eligible for commissary privileges. He or she may, on approval of the local Installation Commander, let an agent make purchases under certain circumstances. Purchases may be used by all members of the family living in the house.

Base Exchange Privileges: Subject to the Installation Commander's determination of availability, the Base Exchange offers various services and facilities, depending on the base's population and what's available from the local civilian sector, such as theaters, barber shops, service stations, clothing stores, dry cleaning, optical shops, package stores, and other sales stores. The unmarried surviving spouse is eligible for base exchange services or, on approval of the installation commander, an agent may be allowed to make purchases under certain circumstances.

Emergency Financial Assistance: The Air Force Aid Society (AFAS), Army Relief Fund (usually co-located with the Army Community Service Activity), or Navy Relief Fund offers qualifying family members financial assistance in the form of interest-free loans or grants during personal and family emergencies. Aid may be given for such purposes as food, rent, utilities, essential car repair, and certain medical and dental care. The assistance is temporary and based on immediate needs. The assistance is available through the AFAS section located in the Family Support Center (FSC) at most Air Force bases. If there is no AFAS office near you, the AFAS has cross-servicing assistance agreements with the American Red Cross, Army Emergency Relief, and the Navy/Marine Corps Relief Society. Ask your CAR for additional details, or contact the base FSC

Income Tax Benefit: You may wish to contact the nearest office of the Internal Revenue Service for information and guidance regarding your federal tax status. Excluded from gross income for income tax purposes are: Social Security benefits; $3,000 of the death gratuity; burial benefits; Veterans Administration pension and compensation payments; property, including cash money received as a gift under will provisions; and face amount of all life insurance policies.

Commercial Insurance Policies: For commercial insurance (policies that you or your spouse purchased from other sources not associated with the military), you should contact the nearest representative or the home office of the company for settlement. Your Casualty Assistance Representative can advise you of any insurance allotments that were being deducted from the member's pay. In addition, any time you purchase commercial life insurance make sure that the policy will pay in the event of death as a result of war (declared or undeclared), aviation accident or suicide. Many commercial policies have war clauses, aviation clauses, and suicide clauses that state the policy is void if the policy holder is killed as a result of war, aviation accident or suicide. Avoid these policies. Have the insurance agent show you in the policy that the policy will pay in these events!

Required Documents: In some cases (insurance companies, banks, credit accounts, etc.) may require you to provide *certified* copies of death certificates, marriage certificates, powers of attorney, etc. So be sure that you request multiple copies of these documents.

VA Home Loan: An un-remarried spouse of a service member who died from a service-connected injury or illness may be eligible for a government-insured home loan benefit. To determine your eligibility, apply to the nearest Veterans Administration Office.

Bank Accounts: Credit Unions, Bank and Charge Accounts: Contact all financial institutions concerning transfer of accounts to the survivor's name. Also ask about any insurance associated with the accounts.

Gold Star Lapel Pin: You may be eligible for this Lapel Pin. The pin is usually presented to the next of kin of service members who lost their lives while engaged in an action against an enemy of the United

THE MILITARY SPOUSE

States, or while serving with a friendly foreign force. Contact your Casualty Assistance Representative to obtain a gold star lapel button.

Gold Star Wives Of America, Inc: A non-profit national military widows service organization that provides support and information to widows of service members who die on active duty or as a result of service-connected disabilities. They respond to all non-monetary requests for assistance. For additional information or assistance, you may write to: The Gold Star Wives of America, Inc., P.O. Box 361986, Birmingham, Alabama 35236, or call them toll free at 1-888-751-6350.

Military Funeral Support: The Department of Defense Directive 1300.15, Military Funeral Support, establishes three distinct categories of veterans and the level of military burial honors each category minimally receives. The three categories are:

- Those who die on active duty or were awarded the Medal of Honor receive, upon request, full military honors: casket bearers, firing party, officer or noncommissioned officer in charge, bugler, and chaplain, if requested.

- Those who retired from military service receive full honors, if requested and **resources permitting**. At a minimum, a service representative will attend the interment service and present the interment flag to the next of kin.

- Those who were honorably discharged may have a service representative, if requested and **resources permitting**, who will attend the interment service and present the interment flag to the next of kin.

- The next of kin or appropriate individual must request the funeral honors, they are not provided automatically. Department of Defense (DoD) policy calls for the funeral directors, rather than the next of kin, to contact the military.

PATRICIA GERECHT & MARK GERECHT

- This toll free number 1-877-MIL-HONR (645-4667) has been set up for funeral directors to coordinate the ceremonies. DoD has established a Web site which explains the funeral honors process: http://www.militaryfuneralhonors.osd.mil

Frequently Asked Questions Concerning Military Funerals:

Q. How can I quickly find out the status of the headstone ordered for my spouse's grave?

A. The National Cemetery Administration maintains a single, nationwide, toll-free telephone number to make it easier for veterans and their families to inquire about the VA headstone and marker program. The number, 1-800-697-6947, connects callers to the VA's National Cemetery Administration Office of Memorial Programs in Washington, D.C., Mon. through Fri., 8:00 a.m. to 5:00 p.m. (EST).

Q: Who pays for the military headstone?

A: The military will pay for a standard military headstone.

Q. My spouse is buried in a national cemetery that is now closed. We always planned to be buried together. What can I do?

A. Even a "closed" national cemetery will be able to accommodate the burial of the spouse of someone already interred in the cemetery. "Closed" means lack of space prevents the cemetery from accepting full casketed burials of those without a spouse already buried in the cemetery.

Q. My first spouse passed away a few years ago and is buried in Arlington National Cemetery based on my eligibility. I have since remarried. Will my current spouse also be eligible to be buried in Arlington? (this situation pertains to a service member that is living and

THE MILITARY SPOUSE

their non service member spouse dies before them)

A. Yes. Your remains and those of your previous and current spouses may be buried in the same grave site.

Q. What are the VA burial benefits?

A. Your surviving spouse should know that the VA will pay allowances toward your burial expenses up to the following amounts:

- $300 burial allowance when burial is in a private or national cemetery.
- $300 plot or interment allowance if burial is in a private cemetery.
- $2,000 allowance if cause of death is service-connected. Payable if internment is in a private or national cemetery. When this is authorized, the $300 burial allowance and/or the $300 plot allowance is not payable.

Q. Am I eligible for VA burial benefits?

A. You may be eligible for a VA burial allowance if:

- you paid for a related veteran's burial or funeral and
- you have not been reimbursed by another government agency or some other source, such as the deceased veteran's employer and
- the veteran was discharged under conditions other than dishonorable.

In addition, at least one of the following conditions must be met:

- the veteran died because of a service-related disability OR
- the veteran was receiving VA pension or compensation at the time of death OR
- the veteran was entitled to receive VA pension or compensation but decided not to reduce his/her military retirement or disability pay OR

- the veteran died in a VA hospital, in a nursing home under VA contract, or in an approved state nursing home.

Q. What is the Presidential Memorial Certificate (PMC) Program?

A. The PMC Program was started by President John F. Kennedy in March 1962 to honor the memory of honorably discharged, deceased veterans. This program has continued with all subsequent presidents. The certificate, which bears the president's signature, expresses the country's grateful recognition of the veteran's service in the armed forces. The PMC program is administered by the VA. Eligible recipients, or someone acting on their behalf, may apply for a PMC in person at any VA regional office or by U.S. mail only. Requests cannot be sent via email. There is no form to use when requesting a PMC. Please be sure to enclose a copy of the veteran's discharge and death certificate. Please submit copies only; original documents cannot be returned. If you would like to request a PMC, or if you requested one more than eight (8) weeks ago and have not received it yet, either:

- Fax your request and all supporting documents (copy of discharge and death certificate) to: (202) 565-8054, or
- Mail your request and all supporting documents using the U.S. Postal Service or a commercial mail service, such as one of the overnight or express mail delivery services, to:

Presidential Memorial Certificates (41A1C)
Department of Veterans Affairs
810 Vermont Ave., N.W.
Washington, DC 20420-0001

If you have questions about a certificate you have received, a request you have already sent in, or about the program in general, call (202) 565-4964 or e-mail PMC@mail.va.gov.

For more information, contact Mortuary Affairs and Casualty Support Division: (703) 325-5304 or (703) 325-5314.

THE MILITARY SPOUSE

Requesting Replacement Medals: The Standard Form (SF) 180, Request Pertaining to Military Records, is recommended for requesting medals and awards. Provide as much information as possible, make sure you specifically request medal/decoration replacement in the remarks, and send the form to the appropriate address below:

Army: National Personnel Records Center
Medals Section (NRPMA-M)
9700 Page Avenue
St. Louis, MO 63132-5100

Air Force (including Army Air Corps & Army Air Forces),National Personnel Records Center
Air Force Reference Branch (NRPMF)
9700 Page Avenue
St. Louis, MO 63132-5100

Navy/Marine Corps/Coast Guard Bureau of Naval Personnel Liaison Office
Room 5409
9700 Page Avenue
St. Louis, MO 63132-5100

Where the Medals are Mailed From:

Army: U.S. Army Soldier & Biological Chemical Command, IMMC
Soldier Systems Directorate
700 Robbins Avenue
P.O. Box 57997
Philadelphia, PA 19111-7997

Air Force: Headquarters, Air Force Personnel Ctr
AFPC/DPPPR
550 C Street West, Suite 12
Randolph AFB, TX 78150-4714

Navy/Marine Corps/Coast Guard: Bureau of Naval Personnel Liaison Office
Room 5409
9700 Page Avenue
St. Louis, MO 63132-5100

Where to Write for Problems/Appeals:

Army: Commander PERSCOM
Attn: TAPC-PDO-PA
200 Stovall Street
Alexandria, VA 22332-0471

Air Force: Headquarters Air Force Personnel Ctr
AFPC/DPPPR
550 C Street West, Suite 12
Randolph AFB, TX 78150-4714

Navy: Chief of Naval Operations
(OPNAV 09B33)
Awards & Special Projects
Washington, DC 20350-2000

Marine Corps: Commandant of the Marine Corps
Military Awards Branch (MMMA)
3280 Russell Road
Quantico VA 22134-5100

Coast Guard: Commandant U.S. Coast Guard
Medals and Awards Branch
(PMP-4)
Washington, DC 20593-0001

CHAPTER 12
HOW TO VOICE YOUR CONCERNS, OPINIONS, COMPLAINTS AND BE HEARD

Usually spouses or service members who are having problems just want to be heard (perhaps just to vent) and be provided a reasonable degree of comfort that their issue has been addressed. This chapter will focus on how you as an individual will increase your chances of having your issue received in a positive manner by members of the chain of command. This chapter will also outline courses of action that are available to you should the initial steps fail.

Attitude and Tone:

The most important aspect of voicing your concern is to ensure you have the **right attitude and tone**. By this we mean:

- Be calm and even-tempered.

- Don't be emotional and/or demanding.

- Don't try to intimidate the chain of command.

Using the wrong attitude and tone will cause you and the chain of command a lot of heartburn and hard feelings. In the end nobody wins .

Goals:

Your 1st goal should be to have your concern heard by the appropriate agency or person and for them to participate as an active listener. Your 2nd goal should be to gain credibility with the individual you are talking with in order to resolve the issue in a factual, courteous and professional manner. Approaching someone with the wrong attitude and tone (being emotional, making unrealistic demands, etc.) will not help you resolve the issue quicker, and it will not help you in dealing with individuals in the future. The Army Family Action Plan (AFAP), is a great tool for getting issues that may affect the whole military community resolved. These are issues that people in the community point out that are then addressed at the installation level, and eventually some are presented to the senior leaders of the Army for resolution. The installation program usually culminates in a 2 or 3 day work shop at each installation on an annual basis. *Our sister services may also have a similar mechanism for resolving issues.*

Steps To Resolving A Concern Or Complaint:

- Identify what the exact concern or problem is. Be able to write it down in a short sentence, providing all pertinent details.

- Know what type of resolution or solution you want. Most leaders will ask you "What would you like me to do?" Or "What do you see as a workable solution?" By having a workable solution you have started to establish credibility.

- **Do your research:** Find out what regulation, manual, or reference covers the area you are voicing your concern over. Read it and understand it. If the military is doing it, you can bet there is a reference to cover it!

    o Look for **key words** in the reference that may **provide** you or the other party **latitude** to make decisions. These can work for or against you depending on your concern. Keywords in this category will be words like: **could, should, may, can, commander's discretion, etc.**

    o Also look for **key words** that are **fixed or required actions**. These would be words like: **will, will not, requires approval from a higher authority, must, cannot, etc.** These words leave little doubt that an action must or must not occur. Again

THE MILITARY SPOUSE

depending on your concern these words can help or hurt your case.

- If you believe or perceive that the desired outcome is not a workable solution (under the current rules), you may ask or request what is commonly known as *an exception to policy*. In some cases Commanders at various levels can grant an exception to policy depending on the issue and the reference governing the issue.

    o **How does an exception work?** Here is an example - Let's say because of ill health one of your parents is coming to live with you for a period of time to exceed 30 days and you are living in post quarters. The current housing policy states that a guest or guests can only reside in quarters for no more than 30 days. In this situation you would lay out the facts and circumstances of the case and request that your family member be allowed to stay "for either a specified period of time, for example, 90 days or an indefinite period of time, based on the illness." If you are granted a specified exception (for example 90 days), than prior to the expiration date you can apply for another exception or your family member(s) must leave.

In summary, be sure you:

- Know what the concern is.

- Provide a list of solutions that would satisfy you.

- Do your homework by researching.

- Have a fall-back plan with a request for an exception to policy. (If this is a reasonable/rational request, given the situation.)

*** **Understand that in some cases a Commander cannot legally, ethically, or morally, make an exception to policy, regulation, etc.**

- Next find out who you should speak with. Usually you should start at the lowest level of the command. These are the individuals who may have the most knowledge about a situation and the facts bearing on the case. If you go around them you set the wrong attitude and tone. In addition when you speak with someone higher in the chain of command they must in turn go back to the lowest level and get their side of the issue before they can give you an answer.

    Note: There are times in which you may feel uncomfortable discussing an issue with the chain of command or in which you believe that using the chain of command may result in retribution or hardship. In these extreme cases it may be appropriate to seek resolution at a higher level or from an external agency. Please keep in mind these cases are *extremely rare*. In addition, *most Commanders/Leaders want to do the right thing and will aggressively try to assist you in obtaining your goal. They usually want to resolve an issue quickly and in the right way.*

- If you do not receive a satisfactory answer you can choose to continue voicing your concern up the chain of command until you receive what you believe to be a reasonable answer, the decision is explained to your satisfaction (even though you may not like the answer), or you are determined to correct what you honestly believe to be an injustice or unfair policy.

- Once you have exhausted your efforts in the chain of command you can take your concerns to other agencies on post or within the Army. These agencies are specifically available for resolving issues and complaints. They include:

    - The Local Inspector General's Office (IG).

    - The Local Judge Advocate General (Legal Office).

    - The Local Equal Opportunity Office (EO/EEO).

THE MILITARY SPOUSE

- o The Post Commander may also have a hotline established for individual to call with their concerns, issues, or suggestions.

Note: Each office listed above also has a Department of the Army (DA) office as well. You may choose to utilize this office. However, be sure that you understand the process. For example: if you took your complaint to the Department of the Army Inspector General's office (DAIG). They would take your complaint with all the details you provide and turn the case over to the installation Inspector General to investigate. Once the installation completes their investigation they will report the findings back to DAIG and they would in turn report back to you. There is a time and place for such complaints but in reality the problem goes back to the lowest level to be resolved, so why not start there. If you have to go forward you can show that you have placed faith in the system and utilized the process as it was designed to be used. An IG complaint is a serious issue, so be sure that the issue you are raising is valid and serious, make sure you have your facts straight.

Other Channels for Resolution: These courses of action are only used as a last resort, during an emergency or extreme issue.

- o Writing a letter to your Congressional Representative.
- o Writing a letter to your Senator.

Note: In these letters explain the problem, what you would like to see as a solution, the actions you have taken to try and resolve the problem at your level. Be clear and to the point.

There are times when it may be appropriate to go over someone's head to resolve an issue. These would be cases in which it is obvious that someone is not being responsive, is blatantly not adhering to a regulation, instruction, or policy, has been unprofessional, etc. However it is important to remember that you should ensure that your decision to take it higher is clearly based on the facts and not emotion.

Most importantly, treat others like you want to be treated. This is perhaps the most important aspect of the process. It will almost always ensure cooperation at the lowest level, enhance your credibility, and allow you to be viewed as a reasonable individual.

Do:

- Identify the issue, concern or problem.

- Know what type of resolution you want.

- Be prepared to request an exception to policy if applicable.

- Research the reference for facts and look for keywords.

- Attempt to resolve the problem at the lowest level.

- Go up the chain of command or to an external agency if you are not satisfied with the quality of the response you receive.

- Ensure you treat others like you want to be treated.

- Be factual.

- Keep the conversation as positive as possible (attitude and tone).

Avoid:

- Being seen as someone:
    - Who constantly complains
    - Who cannot be satisfied
    - Unreasonable
    - Emotional
    - Who shoots straight to the top to solve an issue

THE MILITARY SPOUSE

- Threatening statements like, "I'm going over your head...I'm going straight to the top...I'll have your job, etc." These comments set a negative tone and put the person you are speaking with on the defense. Odds are that individual you are speaking with has some degree of validity to their response. Threats are not usually taken seriously because usually **(there are exceptions)** the person you are dealing with **believes or knows** they are correct in their response. *Threatening statements only take away from your credibility and show you as emotional.*

Common Sense Check: A final note, you must make the determination of when to stop raising an issue. The phrase "the squeaky wheel gets the oil" is a true expression but ask yourself the following questions:

- Is my request reasonable?

- Did I receive a reasonable response?

- Is this concern/issue worth continuing up the chain of command?

- Is this concern/issue a battle I really need to fight?

- Are you fighting this battle on someone else's behalf? If so why aren't they fighting it? Should you really be fighting this battle? Are you championing to someone else's cause? *If your answer is "yes" than you probably need to re-evaluate.*

If you answered "yes" to the above questions *(except the last, your answer should always be NO to the last question)*. Then continue to pursue your concern. In some rare cases you must be persistent to get an issue resolved. Perhaps your persistence may not help your situation but perhaps it will help those that have the same issue later. Maintain your faith and confidence in the chain of command; they will normally solve your problem quickly.

Family Support Chain: When problems involve the non military spouse, give the Family Readiness Group a chance to work the problem. The Family Readiness Group leader or the Reserves also have Family Readiness Liaison Personnel or a Unit Administrator. These individuals have direct contact with the chain of command and can usually solve problems quickly. Allow these individuals the opportunity to try and solve the problem first especially in a deployment situation.

CHAPTER 13
IMPORTANT WEBSITES & OTHER SUPPORT AGENCIES

Note: Please understand we do not endorse any of these sites. These sites were found and appeared to offer pertinent information concerning subjects that may be of value to military members (active, retired, guard, and reserve). We caution all users to verify authenticity and creditability of the information contained on these sites. Prior to providing any personal information or financial information verify that the sites are operating in good faith. In addition websites change frequently. If you cannot locate a site we suggest that you utilize a search engine such as Google to locate the site.

Note: Be cautious of sites you visit and critically evaluate all sites that are not official military or government sites. Are the sites you visit an individual's opinion? Do they offer official information? Also be careful of information that may be sensitive in nature, or information that could be used by our enemies against us. It is best to avoid posting or providing personal information or information concerning specific units. *Remember, websites other than official sites can provide great information and break things down, or help us understand the process or system of a specific issue better….just remember, they are not official sites and you need to evaluate them carefully before providing information or making a decision based off of their guidance or recommendations.*

Note: Try typing the following into internet search engines for some possible ideas or information: *military wife, military spouse, military regulations…* or be service specific like: *army spouse, etc.*

AKO Account For Your Spouse: Go to the Army AKO site and follow the prompts for a spouse account or use a Google search and type in AKO account for your spouse. Normally you will be taken to a site will provide you with the necessary steps to set up your spouse with an AKO account. It is a great tool and will help them stay up to date on many issues and even be able to download some great tools.

Army Regulations: www.usapa.army.mil. Download Army regulations. For everything that happens in the military there is a regulation that governs it. If you have a question about an issue ask yourself, "What Army Regulation governs the situation?" Look up and read the regulation for yourself. Be armed with the facts.

Army Families Online: http://www.armyfamiliesonline.org.

Army Legal Services: Great website on how to prepare you and your family for numerous legal situations:

- *Department of Defense under "Family Law Matters."* at: https://www.jagcnet.army.mil/Legal

- *Army JAG Website*: http://www.jagc.army.mil/

Benefits and Entitlements:

- https://www.hrc.army.mil/site/Active/TAGD/CMAOC/NavigationPages/nav_benefitsentitlements.htm

Child Support Issues:

- Reservists and Recently Activated Soldiers with Issues Concerning Child Support: State Child Support Enforcement Agencies at: http://www.acf.hhs.gov/programs/cse/extinf.htm

- OCSE Information Memorandum (IM)-01-09 at: http://www.dfas.mil/garnishment/retiredmilitary/im-01-09.pdf

THE MILITARY SPOUSE

Chief Of Chaplain's Office: http://www.chapnet.army.mil/

Deployment Link: http://deploymentlink.osd.mil/. Covers various subjects including Deployment Health Support.

Divorce Information for Military: *http://www.military-divorce-guide.com*

Employment Readiness:

- *Career Jorunal.com:* http://www.careerjournal.com/salaryhiring/

- *My Army Life Too Employment*: www.Myarmylifetoo.com
    - Unemployment compensation
    - Resume services
    - Employment bulletin board

- **Military Spouse Network:** http://www.mscn.org. Covers information to help military spouses find jobs and employers that are interested in hiring military spouses.

- **Military Spouse:** http://www.milspouse.org/

- **Military Spouse Preference Eligibility Wizard:** http://cpolrhp.belvoir.army.mil/eur/employment/msp/index.asp?Try=Yes

- **Job Fair Listing:** http://www.acap.army.mil/transitioner/job_fairs/index.cfm

- **Salary Calculator:** http://www.homefair.com/homefair/calc/salcalc.html. Calculates what you will need to make and to maintain the same standard of living in another location.

- **Salary.com:** http://swz.salary.com/. Know what your worth at the low, middle, and high end of your profession down to your zip code area. Utilize the free report.

Employer Support for the Guard and Reserve: www.ESGR.com. Employer Support for the Guard and Reserve (ESGR) is a Department of Defense organization. It is a staff group within the Office of the Assistant Secretary of Defense for Reserve Affairs (ASD/RA), which is in itself a part of the Office of the Secretary of Defense.

Finances:

- **Investing:**

    - *Drip Advisor:* http://www.dripadvisor.com

    - *My Money:* www.mymoney.gov. A good site on a wide variety of money matters.

- **Military pay questions including:**

    - *Normal Pay, Retired Pay, Annuities, Garnishments, Child Support, etc*: http://www.dod.mil/dfas/

    - *Military Retirement Calculators:* http://www.defenselink.mil/militarypay/retirement/index.html

Homeowners Assistance Program: http://hap.usace.army.mil/

Identity Theft:

- Federal Trade Commission: www.consumer.gov/idtheft

THE MILITARY SPOUSE

- FBI Internet Fraud Complaint Center: http://www.ic3.gov/default.aspx

- Privacy Rights Clearing House: www.privacyrights.org

- Identity Theft Resource Center: www.idtheftcenter.org

- Obtain a free copy of your credit report once a year:

    o Annual Free Credit report government sponsored site: http://www.ftc.gov/freereports
    o Trans Union: http://www.transunion.com
    o Experian: www.experian.com
    o Equifax: www.equifax.com

Insurance:

- *SGLI*: http://www.insurance.va.gov. Provides information on SGLI and Family Life Insurance, also provides an insurance calculator.

- *Federal Long Term Health Care*: http://www.opm.gov/insure/ltc. Provides information on long term health care. Can give you an idea of what you may pay.

Mass Mailing Listings Removal:

- *Direct mailing and phone solicitations*: http://www.the-dma.org

Military Acronyms: http://www.militarywords.com/

Military.com: http://www.military.com/spouse

Military Child Education Coalition: http://www.militarychild.org. A non-profit organization that promotes partnership and provides networking of military installations and their supporting school districts.

Military Officers Association of America: http://www.moaa.org. Offers excellent publications on survivor benefits and other related subjects, for retirees and reservists.

Military Funerals Website: http://www.militaryfuneralhonors.osd.mil

Military Benefits: http://www.militarybenefits.com/

Military Records: How to Obtain http://www.archives.gov/research_room/obtain_copies/veterans_service_records.html

Military Ribbons: Professional ultra thin military ribbons for all services: http://www.militaryribbons.net/

Military Spouse: http://www.milspouse.org/

Military Support Sites:

- *Army Community Service*: www.myarmylifetoo.com

- *Army Emergency Relief:* www.aerhq.org

- *Navy Marine Corps Relief Society*: www.nmcrs.org

- *Air Force Aid Society*: www.afas.org

- *Coast Guard Mutual Assistance*: www.cgmahq.org

- *Military Wives And Women*: www.cinchouse.com

- *National Military Family Association*: www.nmfa.org

- *One Source:* Need Help? 24 hrs a day 7 days a week.

THE MILITARY SPOUSE

- o *Military One Source:* http://www.militaryonesource.com/
- o *Army One Source:* www.armyonesource.com
- o *Navy One Source:* www.navyonesource.com

- *Operation Home Front:* www.operationhomefront.org

- *The Military Family Network*: www.Emilitary.org

- *Virtual Family Readiness Group:* http://www.armyfrg.org

Morale Welfare And Recreation: http://www.armymwr.com/

National Do Not Call/Mail Listings: Helps to remove your name from mass calling list and avoid those annoying phone solicitations.

- *National Do Not Call*: www.donotcall.gov

Scams And Fraud Website (Government Sponsored): www.pueblo.gsa.gov. Select "Scams and Fraud" from the navigation bar.

Sexual Offender Website: http://www12.familywatchdog.us/

Soldier Sailors Relief Act Websites: http://www.jag.navy.mil/documents/SSCRA.htm

Still Serving Veterans: http://www.stillservingveterans.org/. Provides counseling, mentoring, careers, education, and support for severely wounded service members and their families in Alabama.

Support For The Grieving:

- *AARP*: http://www.aarp.org/families/grief_loss/

- *Aircraft Casualty Emotional Support Services* (ACCESS):

http://www.accesshelp.org/

- *Bereaved Parents of the USA*: http://www.bereavedparentsusa.org/

- *Center for Loss & Life Transition:* http://www.centerforloss.com/

- *Compassionate Friends:* http://www.compassionatefriends.org/

- *Parents of Murdered Children Inc:* http://www.pomc.org/

- *Sons and Daughters in Touch:* http://www.sdit.org/

- *The National Center for Grieving Children and Families:* http://www.dougy.org/

- *Widow Net:* http://www.widownet.org/

Tragedy Assistance Program For Survivors: TAPS is a non-profit organization and is America's national peer support organization that cares about and supports all "survivors" including spouses, significant others, children, parents, siblings, coworkers, and friends affected by a death in the armed forces. TAPS operates a national toll-free crisis and information line 24-hours a day, 7 days a week with help available through TAPS' Board of Advisors of leading experts in grief, trauma, and critical incident stress. For more information you may write to: Tragedy Assistance Program for Survivors, National Headquarters, 2001 S Street, NW, Suite 300, Washington, DC 20009, or call them toll free at 1-800-959-8277.

TRICARE: http://www.tricare.osd.mil/

US Military.About.com: http://usmilitary.about.com

- *United States Army:* www.army.mil

THE MILITARY SPOUSE

- *United States Marines: www.USMC.mil*

- *United States Navy: www.navy.mil*

- *United States Air Force: www.af.mil*

- *United States Coast Guard: www.uscg.mil*

Pet Friendly Hotels: www.petswelcome.com. Need pet friendly hotels when you travel? This is the site.

Veterans Administration: http://www.va.gov/

PATRICIA GERECHT & MARK GERECHT

THE MILITARY SPOUSE

CHAPTER 14
MILITARY RANK INSIGNIAS OF GRADE

Army, Air Force, Marine Officer Ranks

Rank	Insignia
General of the Army or Air Force No General of the Marines (5 star)	
General (O-10) Marines (Commandant of the Marine Corps)	
Lieutenant General (O-9)	
Major General (O-8)	
Brigadier General (O-7)	
Colonel (O-6)	
Lieutenant Colonel (O-5)	
Major (O-4)	
Captain (O-3)	
1st Lieutenant (O-2)	
2nd Lieutenant (O-1)	

Navy and Coast Guard Officer Ranks

Rank	Insignia
Fleet Admiral Coast Guard has no Fleet Admiral	
Admiral (O-10)	
Vice Admiral (O-9)	
Rear Admiral Upper Half (O-8) Coast Guard Rear Admiral	
Rear Admiral Lower Half (O-7) Coast Guard Rear Admiral	
Captain (O-6)	
Commander (O-5)	
Lieutenant Commander (O-4)	

THE MILITARY SPOUSE

Lieutenant (O-3)	
Lieutenant Junior Grade (O-2)	
Ensign (O-1)	

Army Warrant Officer Ranks

Rank	Insignia
Chief Warrant Officer 5	
Chief Warrant Officer 4	
Chief Warrant Officer 3	
Chief Warrant Officer 2	
Warrant Officer 1	

Navy Warrant Officer Ranks

Rank	Insignia
Chief Warrant Officer 4	
Chief Warrant Officer 3	
Chief Warrant Officer 2	
Chief Warrant Officer 1	

Marine Warrant Officer Ranks

Rank	Insignia
Chief Warrant Officer 5	
Chief Warrant Officer 4	
Chief Warrant Officer 3	
Chief Warrant Officer 2	
Warrant Officer 1	

THE MILITARY SPOUSE

Coast Guard Warrant Officer Ranks

Rank	Insignia
Chief Warrant Officer 4	
Chief Warrant Officer 3	
Chief Warrant Officer 2	
Chief Warrant Officer 1	

Army Enlisted Ranks

Rank	Insignia
Sergeants Major of the Army (E-9)	
Command Sergeants Major (E-9)	
Sergeants Major (E-9)	
First Sergeant (E-8)	
Master Sergeant (E-8)	
Sergeant First Class (E-7)	
Staff Sergeant (E-6)	
Sergeant (E-5)	
Corporal (E-4)	
Specialist (E-4)	
Private First Class (E-3)	
Private Second Class (E-2)	
Private (E-1)	No Insignia

THE MILITARY SPOUSE

Air Force Enlisted Ranks

Rank	Insignia
Chief Msgt of The Air Force (E-9)	
Command Chief Master Sergeant (E-9)	
First Sergeant (E-9)	
Chief Master Sgt (E-9)	
First Sergeant(E-8)	
Senior Master Sgt (E-8)	
First Sergeant (E-7)	
Master Sergeant (E-7)	
Technical Sergeant (E-6)	
Staff Sergeant (E-5)	
Senior Airman (E-4)	
Airman First Class (E-3)	
Airman (E-2)	
Airman Basic (E-1)	No Insignia

199

PATRICIA GERECHT & MARK GERECHT

Marine Enlisted Ranks

Rank	Insignia
Sergeants Major of the Corps (E-9)	
Sergeants Major (E-9)	
Master Gunnery Sergeant (E-9)	
First Sergeant (E-8)	
Master Sergeant (E-8)	
Gunnery Sergeant (E-7)	
Staff Sergeant (E-6)	
Sergeant (E-5)	
Corporal (E-4)	
Lance Corporal (E-3)	
Private First Class (E-2)	
Private (E-1)	No Insignia

THE MILITARY SPOUSE

Navy Enlisted Ranks

Rank	Insignia
Mst. Chief Petty Officer Of The Navy (E-9)	
Master Chief Petty Officer (E-9)	
Senior Chief Petty Officer (E-8)	
Chief Petty Officer (E-7)	
Petty Officer 1st Class (E-6)	
Petty Officer 2nd Class (E-5)	
Petty Officer 3rd Class (E-4)	
Seaman (E-3)	
Seaman Apprentice (E-2)	
Seaman Recruit (E-1)	

201

Coast Guard Enlisted Ranks

Rank	Insignia
Master Chief Petty Officer Of The C.G. (E-9)	
Command Master Chief Petty Officer (E-9)	
Master Chief Petty Officer (E-9)	
Senior Chief Petty Officer (E-8)	
Chief Petty Officer (E-7)	
Petty Officer 1st Class (E-6)	
Petty Officer 2nd Class (E-5)	
Petty Officer 3rd Class (E-4)	
Airman (E-3)	
Fireman (E-3)	
Seaman (E-3)	

THE MILITARY SPOUSE

Airman Apprentice (E-2)			
Fireman Apprentice (E-2)			
Seaman Apprentice (E-2)			
Seaman, Fireman, Airman Recruit	No Insignia		

PATRICIA GERECHT & MARK GERECHT

THE MILITARY SPOUSE

PATRICIA GERECHT & MARK GERECHT

THE MILITARY SPOUSE

PATRICIA GERECHT & MARK GERECHT

Other publications available from

MENTOR ENTERPRISES, INC.
7910 Memorial Parkway SW, Suite F-1
Huntsville, Alabama 35802
info@mentorenterprisesinc.com

Books

THE MENTOR: *Everything You Need To Know About Leadership and Counseling.*

THE TRAINER: *A Training Guide for All Ranks.*

THE EVALUATOR: *A Comprehensive Guide for Preparing NCOER Evaluation Reports.*

THE WRITER: *A comprehensive guide for writing awards.*

Wear It Right! Army Uniform Book: *Answer your army uniform questions instantly!*

Digital Products

Award Quick: *Helps you quickly and accurately write the awards your soldiers deserve. Includes citations, achievement statements, forms, and much more.*

Counsel Quick: *Innovative software that includes all the forms, examples, and references you will need to quickly compose and manage US Army counseling statements.*

Counsel Quick Vol. 1: *Places special emphasis on counseling typically conducted by first line leaders.*

Counsel Quick Vol. 2: *Places special emphasis on counseling typically conducted by senior leaders.*

Counsel Quick Vol. 3: *Even more counseling templates and references! Available July 2009.*

Rater Quick: *Contains the latest forms, examples, and references you will need to quickly compose and manage professional looking Evaluation Reports all in one easy to use program. We offer both OER and NCOER versions of this software.*

Also available online at www.gipubs.com.